AF556249

RECESSION HIT MANAGEMENT

RECESSION HIT MANAGEMENT

Edited by

Rajib Lochan Panigrahy
Faculty (MBA)
Ambedkar College of Management &
Technology Berhampur
(Orissa)

&

Anil Kumar Sahu
Reader (MBA)
Department of Business Administration
Berhampur University
Berhampur
(Orissa)

DISCOVERY PUBLISHING HOUSE PVT. LTD.
NEW DELHI-110 002

Published by:
Tilak Wasan
DISCOVERY PUBLISHING HOUSE PVT. LTD.
4831/24, Prahlad Street, Ansari Road
Darya Ganj, New Delhi-110002 (India)
Phone: +91-11-23279245, 43764432
Fax: +91-11-23253475
E-mail: parul.wasan@gmail.com
info@discoverypublishinggroup.com
web: www.discoverypublishinggroup.com

***First Edition:* 2011**
ISBN: 978-81-8356-821-0

Recession Hit Management

Printed at:
Shree Balaji Art Press
Delhi

Preface

A *global recession* is a period of global economic slowdown. The International Monetary Fund (IMF) takes many factors into account when defining a global recession, but it states that global economic growth of three per cent or less is "equivalent to a global recession". By this measure, three periods since 1985 qualify: 1990-1993, 1998 and 2001-2002. Julius Shiskin suggested several rules of thumb to identify a recession, which included two successive quarterly declines in Gross Domestic Product (GDP), a measure of the nation's output. This two-quarter metric is now a commonly held definition of a recession. In the United States, the National Bureau of Economic Research (NBER) is regarded as the authority which identifies a recession and which takes into account several measures in addition to GDP growth before making an assessment. In many developed nations other than USA, the two-quarter rule is also used for identifying a recession. Whereas a national recession is identified by two quarters of decline, defining a *global recession* is more difficult, because developing nations are expected to have a higher GDP growth than developed nations. The world growth is projected to slow from five per cent in 2007 to 3.75 per cent in 2008 and to just over two per cent in 2009. Most mainstream economists believe that recessions are caused by inadequate aggregate demand in the economy, and favour the use of expansionary macro-economic policy during recessions.

The global economy is beginning to pull out of a recession unprecedented in the post-World War II era, but stabilization is uneven and the recovery is expected to be sluggish. Economic growth during 2009-10 is now projected to be about

½ percentage points higher than projected in the April 2009 [World Economic Outlook (WEO)], reaching 2.5 per cent in 2010. Accordingly, global activity is forecast to contract by 1.4 per cent in 2009 and to expand by 2.5 per cent in 2010, which is 0.6 percentage point higher than envisaged in the April 2009. The higher annual average growth rate for 2010 largely reflects carry-over from a mark-up in growth during the final half of 2009. On a fourth-quarter-over-fourth-quarter basis, real GDP growth is projected at 2.9 per cent in 2010, compared with 2.6 per cent in the April, (WEO) forecast.

Monetarists would favour the use of expansionary monetary policy, while Keynesian economists may advocate increased government spending to spark economic growth. Supply-side economists may suggest tax cuts to promote business capital investment. Laissezfaire minded economists may simply recommend that the government not interfere with natural market forces. Some recessions have been anticipated by stock market declines. In stocks for the long-run, Siegel mentions that since 1948, ten recessions were preceded by a stock market decline, by a lead time of 0 to 13 months (average 5.7 months), while ten stock market declines of greater than 10 per cent. The real-estate market also usually weakens before a recession. However, real-estate declines can last much longer than recessions. Since the business cycle is very hard to predict, Siegel argues that it is not possible to take advantage of economic cycles for timing investments. Even the NBER takes a few months to determine if a peak or trough has occurred in the United States. During an economic decline, high yield stocks such as fast moving consumer goods (FMCG), pharmaceuticals, and tobacco tend to hold up better.

The IMF estimates that global recessions seem to occur over a cycle lasting between 8 and 10 years. During what the IMF terms the past three global recessions of the past three decades, global per capita output growth was zero or negative. The world is still wrestling with the deepest global recession since the 1930s. Most financial markets are once again perky, but GDP in most countries is at best growing slowly and unemployment rates are still increasing. Economic forecasters have shown themselves to be totally unreliable and the signs of recovery are tentative. But it is not too soon to draw three financial-economic lessons from the crisis. First, imbalances matter. The increasingly imbalanced relations of asset prices and incomes proved at least as hazardous. Second, debt is dangerous. Central banks, investment bankers and politicians all signed up to the cult of debt. But companies that went for balance-sheet "efficiency" - often piling on debt simply to fund share buybacks and huge mortgages were caught out. Third, globalization doesn't work by itself. Free movement of capital has facilitated rapid shifts in cross-border capital flows, currency values and prices of commodities. Economies benefited when they were jerked up, but were left vulnerable to painful disruptions. The three lessons can be boiled down to one: over-stimulated finance leads to economic woe. While trade imbalances have shrunk, governments and central banks are pushing the limits of fiscal and monetary stimulation.

Migrants increasingly vulnerable due to global recession, says UN trade body, 29 July 2009 – Surging global unemployment triggered by the economic crisis is significantly affecting migrant workers, many of whom have lost their livelihoods and are returning to their home countries. With 60 million people expected to be out of work by year's end, bringing the total number of people pushed out of their jobs by the recession to 240 million, "the crisis will be impacting quite significantly on the flow of migrants," Supachai Panitchpakdi, Secretary-General of the UN Conference on Trade and Development (UNCTAD), said at the start of the one-day gathering in Geneva. The economic downturn has hit construction, manufacturing and other sectors that employ many migrants, he said, adding that women migrants will feel the impact as jobs in health care, education and domestic services shrink. Sha Zukang, head of the UN Department of Economic and Social Affairs (DESA), pointed out that the number of migrants could reach 214 million by 2010, but that the recession has reversed the trend of the rising proportion of women in the migrant workforce.

In this vulnerability of global economic recession, most of the countries in the globe has been drastically affected. Asian countries are developing sharply of which India has been felt slightly inside the country but affected the whole the economic strata with deterioration of the excise duties, export of India made softwares, hardwares, cotton products, migrant labourers/outsourcing, etc. This book contains 13 articles of research on global financial crisis, global meltdown and its impact on several economies and continents, job market/employment and role of HR managers/firms/sectors, financial crisis and its affect investment in banking, financial institutions and non-banking sectors, several aspects of corporate governance for better firm management and employee-stakeholder relation/satisfaction, etc. The themes has been elaborated by the eminent authors/researchers mainly from the faculties of Management, Business Administration, Economics, Commerce of different academic institutions of repute from several parts of India. We owe our deep sense of gratitude to the contributors to make the book self-sufficient and the publisher as a whole to publish the book.

Editors

Contents

List of Contributors

K. Sambasivam, S.S. Lecturer in Economics, The New College, Chennai-14.

Dr. A. Abdul Raheem, S.S. Lecturer in Economics, The New College, Chennai-14.

Dr. Sudhakar Patra, Reader in Economics, Ravenshaw University, Cuttack, Orissa.

Rajesh D. Shelke, Assistant Professor, Department of Agricultural Economics & Statistics, College of Agriculture, Latur, Marathwada Agricultural University, Parbhani, Maharashtra, India.

Mr. Sasikant Tripathy, Lecturer in Finance, DRIEMS B-School, Tangi, Cuttack, Orissa.

Dr. Abdus Shukur, S.S. Lecturer, Dept of Economics, The New College, Chennai-14.

Dr. M. Abdul Jamal, Lecturer, Deptt. of Economics, The New College, Chennai-14.

Dr. P. Muthaiyan, S.S Lecturer in Economics, The New College, Chennai-14.

Dr. Aditya Kumar Patra, Lecturer in Economics, Kalinga Mahavidyalaya, G.Udayagiri, Kandhamal, Orissa-762100.

Dr. A N Shankar, Asst. Professor, Department of Commerce, Mizoram University, Aizawl-796009, Mizoram.

Dr. N M Panda, Professor, Department of Commerce, North-Eastern Hill University, Shillong-793022, Meghalaya.

Mr. Minaketan Dash, Student (MBA), DRIEMS B-School, Tangi, Cuttack, Orissa.

Sthitaprajna Debadutta Samal, Lecturer, Management Studies, MITS Group, Bhubaneswar, Orissa.

Minati Sahoo, Lecturer in Economics, Trident Group of Institutions, Bhubaneswar, Orissa.

Dr. Kabita Kumari Sahu, Lecturer in Economics, North Orissa University, Baripada, Orissa.

Dr. Subhasree Panda, Lecturer, Department of Business Administration, North Orissa University, Baripada, Orissa.

CHAPTER

Current Financial Crisis on Developing Countries : An Overview

K. Sambasivam
Dr. A. Abdul Raheem

ABSTRACT

The global financial crisis is already causing a considerable slowdown in most developed countries. Governments around the world are trying to contain the crisis, but many suggest the worst is not yet over. In the recent growth performance in developed and developing countries, the channels through which the global crisis affects developing countries, which countries might be mostly at risk, and possible policy responses. Therefore, this chapter focuses on the impact of the current financial crisis on developing countries.

Introduction

The global financial crisis is already causing a considerable slowdown in most developed countries. Governments around the world are trying to contain the crisis, but many suggest the worst is not yet over. Stock markets are down more than 40 per cent from their recent highs. Investment banks have collapsed, rescue packages are drawn up involving more than a trillion US dollars, and interest rates have been cut around the world in what looks like a coordinated response. Leading indicators of global economic activity, such as shipping rates, are declining at alarming rates. In the recent growth performance in developed and developing countries, the channels through which the global crisis affects developing countries, which countries might be most at risk, and possible policy responses. Therefore, this paper focuses on the impact of the current financial crisis on developing countries

Growth in Developed and Developing Countries

With a recession already underway in the U.K., Germany, France, the U.S.A. and other developed countries, it is quite startling to hear the Malawian finance minister argue that Malawi's economy is projected to grow by more than eight per cent this year. Yet this is today's stark reality. The U.S.A. is going through the greatest financial crisis since the 1930s, but, as the *Financial Times* has reported, Lagos is not Lehman. Nigeria, held back by decades of economic mismanagement, is growing at nearly nine per cent. Leaders in China suggest that they can help the world by offering growth rates of up to ten per cent, and many African countries still gain significantly from this (they are growing at 6-7%).

Growth performances vary substantially among developed and developing countries. African growth exceeds OECD growth by margins not seen for 25 years; East Asia's growth is diverging as much as it did during the past significant global economic downturn in the early 1990s.

The relationship between OECD, GDP and Africa's GDP has weakened as a result of the emergence of countries such as China, as well as structural changes in African economies. According to the IMF's World Economic Outlook report in April 2008, a decline in world growth of one percentage point would lead to a 0.5 percentage point drop in Africa's GDP, so the effects of global turmoil on Africa (via trade, FDI, aid) would

Table 1.1. World Economic Outlook Projections

Country	Projections				Difference from July 2008 WEO projections	
	2006	2007	2008	2009	2008	2009
U.S.A.	5.1	5.0	3.9	3.9	–0.2	–0.9
Euro area	2.8	2.0	1.6	0.1	0.3	–0.7
U.K.	2.8	2.6	1.3	0.2	–0.4	–0.1
Brazil	2.8	3.0	1.0	-0.1	–0.8	–1.8
Russia	3.8	5.4	5.2	3.5	0.3	–0.5
China	7.4	8.1	7.0	5.5	–0.7	–1.8
India	11.6	11.9	9.7	9.3	–	–0.5
Sub-Saharan Africa	9.8	9.3	7.9	6.9	–0.1	–1.1
Middle East	6.6	6.9	6.1	6.3	–0.5	–0.5
ASEAN-5	5.7	5.9	6.4	5.9	0.2	–0.1
World trade volume	5.7	6.3	5.5	4.9	–0.1	–1.0
APF/MRDE	9.3	7.2	4.9	4.1	–1.2	–1.9

Source: IMF.

be quite high. The correlation between African GDP and World GDP since 1980 is 0.5, but between 2000 and 2007, it was only 0.2. As there have been significant structural changes (and a move into services that were able to withstand competition much better) as well as the rise of China, African growth has temporarily decoupled from OECD GDP. Several Asian countries have built up healthy government reserves, and solid export performance has helped their strong current account position. Latin American countries are currently in a much better fiscal and external position compared to the 1990s, the decade in which several financial crisis struck.

However, there are also several worrying signs. The combination of high food prices and high oil prices has meant that, while the current account of oil and food importers was in balance by 2003, it was in deficit by four per cent in 2007. Inflation has also doubled. Many developing and especially small and African countries are, therefore, in a bad position to face yet another crisis. The terms of trade shock tend to be highest in small importing countries such as Fiji, Dominica, Swaziland. However, African countries such as Kenya, Malawi, Tanzania are projected to have faced terms of trade shocks of greater than 5 per cent of GDP (World Bank paper for the October 2008 Commonwealth Finance Ministers meeting). And there are also signs of a slowdown in Asia, the engine of recent world growth. In the space of a couple of months, the Asian Development Bank (ADB) has revised its forecast for Asian countries downwards by 1-2 percentage points. The IMF growth forecasts have been revised significantly, especially for the UK (–1.8 percentage points down from the last forecast for 2009), but also India (–1.1 percentage points down to 6.9 per cent real GDP growth), and China and Africa (both down by –0.5 percentage points to 9.3 per cent and 6.3 per cent respectively). The magnitude of the crisis will depend on the response of the U.S.A. and E.U. Trillion dollar rescue packages are launched around the world, but while the markets may eventually respond, the U.K. is already in a recession. Its magnitude will depend, in part, on how accommodative monetary policy can be, with the recent interest rate cut a sure sign the authorities are concerned more about the financial crisis than recent inflationary pressures. There is less scope for expansionary fiscal policy – in fact these rescue measures have increased public debt.

Impact of the Current Financial Crisis on Developing Countries

The current financial crisis affects developing countries in two possible ways. First, there could be financial contagion and spillovers for stock markets in emerging markets. The Russian stock market had to stop trading twice; the India stock market dropped by eight per cent in one day at the same time as stock markets in the USA and Brazil plunged. Stock markets across the world—developed and developing—have all dropped substantially since May 2008. We have seen share prices tumble between 12 and 19 per cent in the USA, UK and Japan in just one week, while the MSCI emerging market index fell 23 per cent. This includes stock markets in Brazil, South Africa, India and China. We need to better understand the nature of the financial linkages, how they occur (as they do appear to occur) and whether anything can be done to minimise contagion. Second, the economic downturn in developed countries may also have significant impact on developing countries. The channels of impact on developing countries include:

- **Trade and trade prices**: Growth in China and India has increased imports and pushed up the demand for copper, oil and other natural resources, which has led to greater exports and higher prices, including from African countries. Eventually, growth in China and India is likely to slow down, which will have knock on effects on other poorer countries.
- **Remittances:** Remittances to developing countries will decline. There will be fewer economic migrants coming to developed countries when they are in a

recession, so fewer remittances and also probably lower volumes of remittances per migrant.

- **Foreign direct investment (FDI) and equity investment:** These will come under pressure. While 2007 was a record year for FDI to developing countries, equity finance is under pressure and corporate and project finance is already weakening. The proposed strata takeover of a South African mining conglomerate was put on hold as the financing was harder due to the credit crunch. There are several other examples in India.
- **Commercial lending:** Banks under pressure in developed countries may not be able to lend as much as they have done in the past. Investors are, increasingly, factoring in the risk of some emerging market countries defaulting on their debt, following the financial collapse of Iceland. This would limit investment in such countries as Argentina, Iceland, Pakistan and Ukraine.
- **Aid:** Aid budgets are under pressure because of debt problems and weak fiscal positions, e.g. in the U.K. and other European countries and in the U.S.A. While the promises of increased aid at the Gleneagles summit in 2005 were already off track just three years later, aid budgets are now likely to be under increased pressure.
- **Other official flows:** Capital adequacy ratios of development finance institutions will be under pressure. However these have been relatively high recently, so there is scope for taking on more risks.

Each of these channels needs to be monitored, as changes in these variables have direct consequences for growth and development (Te Velde, 2008, on pro-poor globalisation). Those countries that have done well by participating in the global economy may also lose out most, depending on policy responses, and this is not the time to reject globalisation but to better understand how to regulate and manage the globalisation processes for the benefit of developing countries. The impact on developing countries will vary. It will depend on the response in developed countries to the financial crisis and the slowdown, and the economic characteristics and policy responses, in developing countries.

The list of channels above suggests that the following types of countries are most likely to be at risk (this is a selection of indicators):

- Countries with significant exports to crisis affected countries such as the U.S.A. and E.U. countries (either directly or indirectly). Mexico is a good example;
- Countries exporting products whose prices are affected or products with high income elasticities. Zambia would eventually be hit by lower copper prices, and the tourism sector in Caribbean and African countries will be hit;
- Countries dependent on remittances. With fewer bonuses, Indian workers in the city of London, for example, will have less to remit. There will be fewer migrants coming into the U.K. and other developed countries, where attitudes might harden and job opportunities become more scarce;
- Countries heavily dependent on FDI, portfolio and DFI finance to address their current account problems (e.g. South Africa cannot afford to reduce its interest rate, and it has already missed some important FDI deals);
- Countries with sophisticated stock markets and banking sectors with weakly regulated markets for securities;
- Countries with a high current account deficit with pressures on exchange rates and inflation rates. South Africa cannot afford to reduce interest rates as it needs to attract investment to address its current account deficit. India has seen a devaluation as well as high

inflation. Import values in other countries have already weakened the current account;

- Countries with high government deficits, for example, India has a weak fiscal position which means that they cannot put schemes in place;
- Countries dependent on aid.

While the effects will vary from country to country, the economic impacts could include:

- Weaker export revenues;
- Further pressures on current accounts and balance of payment;
- Lower investment and growth rates;
- Lost employment.

There could also be social effects:

- Lower growth translating into higher poverty;
- More crime, weaker health systems and even more difficulties meeting the Millennium Development Goals.

Conclusion

The current macro-economic and social challenges posed by the global financial crisis require a much better understanding of appropriate policy responses:

- There needs to be a better understanding of what can provide financial stability, how cross-border cooperation can help to provide the public good of international financial rules and systems, and what the most appropriate rules are with respect to development;
- There needs to be an understanding of whether and how developing countries can minimise financial contagion;
- Developing countries will also need to manage the implications of the current economic slowdown - after a period of strong and continued growth in

- Developing countries, which have promoted interest in structural factors of growth, international macro economic management will now move up the policy agenda. Do countries have room to use fiscal and monetary policies?
- Developing countries need to understand the social outcomes and provide appropriate social protection schemes;

There will also be implications for development policy. There will be limits to financial solutions if the problems lie in the real economy, but development finance institutions may be able to take some risks and support investment flows to developing countries, counteracting reductions in other financial flows. Whether DFIs can take higher risks might be informed by past experience, for example by looking at what happened during the Asian financial crisis of the late 1990s. During this period DFI portfolios were riskier, loan losses higher and returns lower than they are at present. And yet this poorer financial performance has not had an adverse affect on institutional credit ratings. The EBRD argued in 2007 that is able to withstand the impact of a major shock with an impact equivalent to 3.5 times the magnitude of the financial crisis in 1998, without a need to call capital; Aid volumes will come under pressure, but there may also be implications for the composition of aid. Should aid be provided to countries with high risks, and how should this be channeled? Are existing IMF and World Bank schemes sufficient for this, as they already need to address balance of payment problems in countries due to high food and oil prices?

REFERENCES

Henry, Peter Blair (2007), "Capital Account Liberalization: Theory, Evidence, and Speculation", *Journal of Economic Literature,* Vol. XLV, December.

International Monetary Fund (2008a), *"Global Financial Stability Report",* October.

IMF (2008b), "World Economic Outlook", October.

Mohan, Rakesh (2006), "Coping With Liquidity Management in India: A Practitioner's View", *Reserve Bank of India Bulletin,* April.

Mohan, Rakesh (2007a), "Development of Financial Markets in India", *Reserve Bank of India Bulletin*, June.

Mohan, Rakesh (2007b), "India's Financial Sector Reforms: Fostering Growth While Containing Risk", *Reserve Bank of India Bulletin*, December.

Prasad, Eswar S., Raghuram G. Rajan and Arvind Subramanian (2007), "Foreign Capital and Economic Growth", *Brookings Papers on Economic Activity,* 1.

Reserve Bank of India (2008), *Annual Policy Statement for the Year 2008-09, April, World Bank* (2008), "Global Development Finance 2008", June.

CHAPTER

Genesis of Global Financial Crisis and Indian Economy

Sudhakar Patra

Global economic situation deteriorated after mid-September, 2008 following the collapse of the top investment banks in the United States. There was a massive choking of credit and a global crash in the stock markets. The disturbance in the American financial market sent waves of economic disturbances through out the world. The global recession is termed in various names such as economic meltdown, slowdown, and economic downturn etc. There is no doubt that global financial crisis started in late 2008 with its epicenter in the financial system of U.S.A. The explosive growth of U.S.A. during last three decades due to deregulation, technological innovation, growing international mobility of capital and unsustained path of growth are the factors behind economic melt down of U.S.A. Most of the advanced countries are already in the grip of recession and the economic outlook for the developing countries including India is decorating rapidly. The falling production, reduction in volume of trade, joblessness and rise in international food prices aggravated the crisis in many countries. The Government of India adopted several stimulus packages and pragmatic policy with additional spending on infrastructure and tax concessions to lessen the adverse effects of global melt down. The Reserve Bank of India moved quickly to improve liquidity capital and to reduce the risk of investment. The drop in real estate and stock prices and job cuts in the employment market, particularly in export oriented industries are the backwash effects of global financial crisis. The falling rupee against dollar, liquidity and confidence are the main problems of crisis in Indian Financial system.

In this context this article highlights the genesis of the crisis , impact and spread of crisis on Indian economy through different channels. The monetary policy responses and fiscal stimulus of government are analyzed with impact on various sectors. Indian economy has several advantages over other countries due to comfortable reserve position, sound and healthy banking system, priority sector lending and social safety net programmes in addressing the adverse impact of global economic crisis. Hence, this article presents degree and spread of global economic crisis with its impact on Indian Economy and responses to mitigate adverse impact on real and financial sectors of our country.

The financial crisis has been erupted in a comprehensive manner on Wall Street; there was some premature triumphalism among Indian policy-makers and media persons. It has been argued that India would be relatively immune to this crisis, because of the "strong fundamentals" of the economy and the supposedly well-regulated banking system. These effects have been most marked among those developing countries where the foreign ownership of banks has been already well advanced, and when U.S.-style financial sectors with the merging of banking and investment functions have been created. The recent crash in the Sensex was not simply an indicator of the impact of international contagion. There have been warning signals and signs of fragility in Indian finance for some time now, and these are likely to be compounded by trends in the real economy.

Genesis of Financial Crisis

The extent of effects of global slowdown will continue or that will pass relatively quickly, like most other post-World War II recessions can not be predicted at this situation. But it is clear that the panic and fear of crisis has reduced substantially and job market has started recovering slowly. The full extent will only become obvious in the years to come. But if we want to avoid future deep financial meltdowns or even of greater magnitude, the root causes of crisis must be addressed properly. There are two critical and related factors created the current crisis. First, profligate lending which allowed many people to buy overpriced properties that they could not, in reality, afford. Second, the existence of excessive land use regulation which helped drive prices up in many of the most impacted markets. Profligate lending all by itself would not likely have produced the financial crisis. It took a toxic connection with excessive land-use regulation. In some metropolitan markets, land use restrictions, such as urban growth boundaries, building moratoria and large areas made off-limits to development propelled house prices to unprecedented levels, leading to severely higher mortgage exposures. On the other hand, where land regulation was not so severe, in the traditionally regulated markets, such as in Texas, Georgia and much of the U.S. Midwest and South there were only modest increases in relative house prices. If the increase in mortgage exposures around the country had been on the order of those sustained in traditionally regulated markets, the financial losses would have been far less. The origin of crisis can be known from following points.

(i) *The International Financial Crisis and Losses in the US Housing Market:* There is general agreement that the U.S. housing bubble was the proximate cause for the most severe financial crisis (in the US) since the Great Depression. This crisis has spread to other parts of the world, if for no other reason than the huge size of the American economy.

(ii) *Profligate Lending and Losses:* Profligate lending, a macro-economic factor, occurred throughout all markets in the United States. The greater availability of mortgage funding predictably led to greater demand for housing, as people who could not have previously qualified for credit received loans ("subprime" borrowers) and others qualified for loans far larger than they could have secured in the past ("prime" borrowers). When over-stretched, sub-prime and prime borrowers were unable to make their mortgage payments, the delinquency and foreclosure rates could not be absorbed by the lenders (and those which held or bought the "toxic" paper). This undermined the mortgage market, leading to the failures of firms like Bear Stearns and Lehman Brothers and the virtual failures of Fannie Mae and Freddie Mac. In this era of interconnected markets, this unprecedented reversal reverberated around the world.

(iii) *Excessive Land-use Regulation Exacerbated Losses:* Profligate lending increased the demand for housing which produced far different results in different metropolitan areas, depending in large part upon the micro-economic factor of land use regulation. In some metropolitan markets, land use restrictions propelled prices and led to severely higher mortgage exposures. On the other hand, where land regulation was not so severe, in the traditionally regulated markets, there were only modest increases in relative house prices. If the increase in mortgage exposures around the country had been on the order of those sustained in traditionally regulated markets, the financial losses would have been far less. Metropolitan markets that have the more liberal and traditional land use regulation experienced little relative increase in housing prices. Unlike the more strongly regulated markets, the traditionally regulated markets permitted a normal supply response to the higher market demand created by the profligate lending. This disparate price performance is evidence of a well established principle of economics in operation—that shortages and rationing lead to higher prices. Among the 50 metropolitan areas with more than 1,000,000 population, 25 have significant land-use restrictions and 25 are more liberally regulated. The markets with liberal land-use regulation were generally able to absorb from the excess of profligate lending at historic price norms while those with restrictive land-use regulation were not. Moreover, the demand was greater in the more liberal markets, not the restrictive markets. Since 2000, population growth has been at least four times as high in the traditional metropolitan markets as in the more regulated markets. The ultimate examples are liberally regulated Atlanta, Dallas-Fort Worth and Houston, the fastest growing metropolitan areas in the developed world with more than 5,000,000 population, where prices have remained within historic norms. Indeed, the more restrictive markets have seen a huge outflow of residents to the markets with traditional land use regulation.

(*v*) *Toxic Mortgages and Excessive Land Use Regulation:* The overwhelming share of the excess increase in US house prices and mortgage exposures relative to incomes has occurred in the restrictive land-use markets. Our analysis of Federal Reserve and US Bureau of the Census data shows that these over-regulated markets accounted for upwards of 80% of "overhang" of an estimated $5.3 billion in overinflated mortgages.

While the current financial crisis would not have occurred without the profligate lending that became pervasive in the United States, land use rationing policies of smart growth clearly intensified the problem and turned what may have been a relatively minor downturn into a global financial meltdown.

IMPACT OF CRISIS ON INDIAN ECONOMY

The global financial crisis has three major impacts on the Indian economy such as (*i*) Economic Downturn, (*ii*) Exposure of banks and (*iii*) Domestic policy. These points are briefly stated below.

Economic Downturn

After a long spell of growth, the Indian economy was experiencing a downturn. Industrial growth has been faltering, inflation remains at double-digit levels, the current account deficit is widening, foreign exchange reserves are depleting and the rupee is depreciating. The last two features can also be directly related to the current international crisis. The most immediate effect of that crisis on India has been an outflow of foreign institutional investment from the equity market. Foreign institutional investors, who need to retrench assets in order to cover losses in their home countries and were seeking havens of safety in an uncertain environment, have become major sellers in Indian markets.

In 2007-08, net FII inflows into India amounted to $20.3 billion. As compared with this, they pulled out $11.1 billion during the first nine-and-a-half months of calendar year 2008, of which $8.3 billion occurred over the first six-and-a-half months of financial year 2008-09 (April 1 to October 16). This has had two effects: in the stock market and in the currency market.

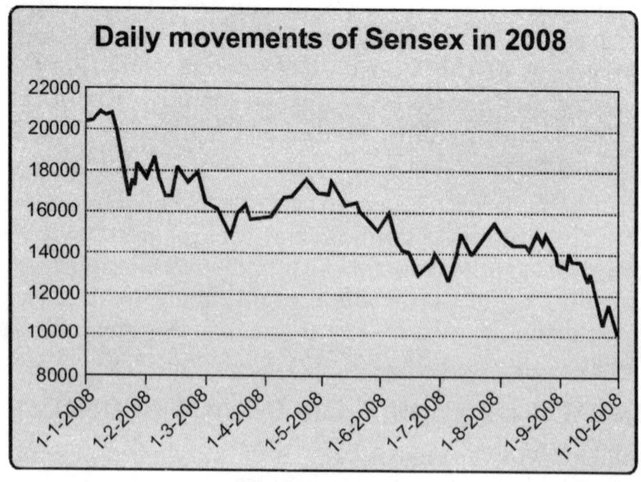

Fig. 2.1.

Given the importance of FII investment in driving Indian stock markets and the fact that cumulative investments by FIIs stood at $66.5 billion at the beginning of this calendar year, the pullout triggered a collapse in stock prices. As a result, the Sensex fell from its closing peak of 20,873 on January 8, 2008, to less than 10,000 by October 17, 2008 (Fig. 2.1).

Falling Rupee

In addition, this withdrawal by the FIIs led to a sharp depreciation of the rupee. Between January 1 and October 16, 2008, the RBI reference rate for the rupee fell by nearly 25 per cent, even relative to a weak currency like the dollar, from Rs 39.20 to the dollar to Rs 48.86 (Fig. 2.2). This was

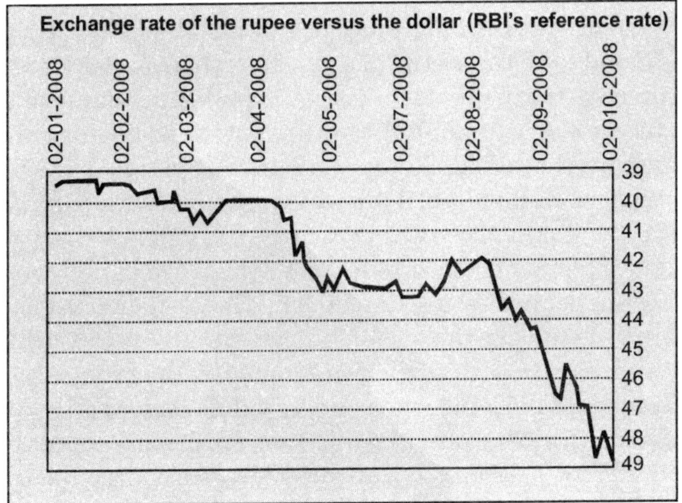

Fig. 2.2

despite the sale of dollars by the RBI, which was reflected in a decline of $25.8 billion in its foreign currency assets between the end of March 2008 and October 3, 2008. It could be argued that the $275 billion the RBI still has in its kitty is adequate to stall and reverse any further depreciation if needed. But given the sudden exit by the FIIs, the RBI is clearly not keen to deplete its reserves too fast and risk a foreign exchange crisis. The result has been the observed sharp depreciation of the rupee. While this depreciation may be good for India's exports that are adversely affected by the slowdown in global markets, it is not so good for those who have accumulated foreign exchange payment commitments. Nor does it assist the Government's effort to rein in inflation.

Exposure of Banks

The global financial crisis could affect India through the second route which is through the exposure of Indian banks or banks operating in India to the impaired assets resulting from the sub-prime crisis. Unfortunately, there were no clear estimates of the extent of that exposure, giving room for rumour in determining market trends. Thus, ICICI Bank was found to be the victim of a run for a short period because of rumours that sub-prime exposure had badly damaged its balance sheet, although these rumours have been strongly denied by the bank. So far the RBI has claimed that the exposure of Indian banks to assets impaired by the financial crisis was small. According to reports, the RBI had estimated that as a result of exposure to collateralized debt obligations and credit default swaps, the combined mark-to-market losses of Indian banks at the end of July was around $450 million. Given the aggressive strategies adopted by the private sector banks, the MTM losses incurred by public sector banks were estimated at $90 million, while that for private banks was around $360 million. As yet these losses are on paper, but the RBI believes that even if they are to be provided for, these banks are well capitalized and can easily take the hit. Such assurances have neither reduced fears of those exposed to these banks or to investors holding shares in these banks. These fears were compounded by those of the minority in metropolitan areas dealing with foreign banks that have expanded their presence in India, whose global exposure to toxic assets must be substantial.

Thirdly, the global crisis and its ripples in India is in the form of the losses sustained by non-bank financial institutions (especially mutual funds) and corporate, as a result of their exposure to domestic stock and currency markets. Such losses were expected to be large, as signaled by the decision of the RBI to allow banks to provide loans to mutual funds against certificates of deposit (CDs) or buyback their own CDs before maturity. These losses are bound to render some institutions fragile, with implications that would become clear only in the coming months

Fourthly, in this uncertain environment, banks and financial institutions concerned about their balance sheets, have been cutting back on credit, especially the huge volume of housing, automobile and retail credit provided to individuals. According to RBI figures, the rate of growth of auto loans fell from close to 30 per cent over the year ending June 30, 2008, to as low as 1.2 per cent. Loans to finance consumer durables purchases fell from around Rs 6,000 crore in the year to June 2007, to a little over Rs. 4,000 crore up to June this year. Direct housing loans, which had increased by 25 per cent during 2006-07, decelerated to 11 per cent growth in 2007-08 and 12 per cent over the year ending June 2008. It is only in an area like credit-card receivables, where banks are unable to control the growth of credit that expansion was, at 43 per cent, quite high over the year ending June 2008, even though it was lower than the 50 per cent recorded over the previous year. It is known that credit-financed housing investment and credit-financed consumption have been important drivers of growth in recent years, and underpin the nine per cent growth trajectory India has been experiencing. The reticence of lenders to increase their exposure in markets to which they are already overexposed and the fears of increasing payment commitments in an uncertain economic environment on the part of potential borrowers are bound to curtail debt-financed consumption and investment. This could slow growth significantly.

Finally, the recession generated by the financial crisis in the advanced economies as a group and the US in particular, will adversely affect India's exports, especially its exports of software and IT-enabled services, more than 60 per cent of which are directed to the US. International banks and financial institutions in the US and EU are important sources of demand for such services, and the difficulties they face will result in some curtailment of their demand. Further, the nationalization of many of these banks is likely to increase the pressure to reduce outsourcing in order to keep jobs in the developed countries. The slowing of growth outside of the financial sector too will have implications for both merchandise and services exports. The net result would be a smaller export stimulus and a widening trade deficit.

Domestic Policy

While these trends are still in process, their effects were already being felt. They were not the only causes for the downturn the economy has been experiencing, but they were found to be important contributory factors. Yet, this does not justify the argument that India's difficulties are all imported. They have been induced by domestic policy as well. The extent of imported difficulties would have been far less if the Government had not increased the vulnerability of the country to external shocks by drastically opening up the real and financial sectors. It is disconcerting; therefore, that when faced with this crisis the Government is not rethinking its own liberalization strategy, despite the backlash against neo-liberalism worldwide. By deciding to relax conditions that apply to FII investments in the vain hope of attracting them back and by focusing on pumping liquidity into the system rather than using public expenditure and investment to stall a recession, it is indicating that it hopes that more of what created the problem would help solve it.

ADVERSE IMPACT ON EMPLOYMENT AND INDUSTRY

The growth rate of industrial production in India was 11.3 per cent in 2007-08 but it decreased to seven per cent in

2008-09 after recession. The performance of both consumer durables and non-durables has dipped. The manufacturing sector was worst hit because growth rate declined from 12.5 per cent in 2006-07 to 8.7 per cent in 2007-08 and further declined. The ripples of recession leading to reduction in export was felt in all developing countries. The low credit availability and reduced export combinely resulted in loss of employment and reduction of income. According to IMF, world output growth came down from five per cent in 2007 to 3.7 per cent in 2008 and further to 2.2 per cent in 2009. It is estimated that total employment was reduced from 16.2 million during Sept, 2008 to 15.7 million during December, 2008. There was a loss of about half a million during a period of three months. About five lakh people were rendered jobless between October,2008 to December, 2008 due to recession. The loss of employment was visible in all major sectors like textile and garment, technology and BPO, automobiles, jewellery, transportation etc. The jems and jewellery sector lost 8.43 per cent of its workforce and followed by metal and textile sector by 2.6 per cent.

It is estimated that 5.7 million Indian workers are working in different countries of the world. Only 19 lakh people from Kerala are working in gulf countries. Due to job cuta in Dubai and gulf after recession , thoU.S.A.nds of people have returned home and remittances have reduced substantially. Andhra Pradesh and Tamil Nadu also had more adverse impact in terms of loss of remittances and return of many workers after recession.

RECESSION AND IT INDUSTRY IN INDIA

Many large global corporations have invested in setting up their back offices and home grown companies have risen to service these requirements. The Indian Big 3 of outsourcing (TCS, Infosys and Wipro) have been rated as being equal to or direct competitors of the Global Big 3 (IBM, HP and Accenture). TCS' takeover of Citibank's BPO e-Serve and Wipro's takeover of Citigroup's IT arm CITOS is a harbinger of things to come. However, the sheen of the outsourcing industry has come under a cloud as a result of the Satyam scandal. But the financial crisis being a reality, momentary caution in the wake of the scandal will give way to business pragmatism. For Indian companies to seize the opportunity that is being offered on a silver platter, they have to look beyond mere off-shoring or near-shoring. The key will be to create a reasonable presence in the buyer's market which will not only enable them to capitalize on proximity to the client but will also allow them to create local employment, earn incentives from the national, state and local governments, market their services for government contracts and most of all, shed the 'India only' tag to become true global services players.

Indian companies need to expand their areas of expertise either through organic or inorganic means after identifying underlying synergies to drive their business strategies. Most importantly, they have to explore possibilities for strategic arrangements with local players who have strong niches. Indian companies need to adopt a consulting oriented client acquisition approach so that they will be able to adequately manage expectation gaps in during the contract lifecycle. Indian companies will have to identify new trends in the outsourcing space and become pioneers as opposed to becoming adopters of patented processes and technologies. This will have to be driven by the company's long term strategy and will have to focus on value co-creation with their clients through the management of their business processes as an approach to building process and technology IP. Finally, Indian companies need adopt new technologies and practice an innovation based delivery process which enables their clients to realize substantial savings while at the same time retaining a competitive advantage in their respective market.

Conclusion

Indian economic scenario is grimmer in 2009 as compared to previous years. But India is not too badly hit by the recession. The Indian economy has globalized rapidly during the past few years. The ratio of exports plus imports to GDP increased by more than 50 per cent between 1997-98 and 2007-08 (from 21.2% to 34.7%). The growth of financial integration has been even more rapid. Three different channels of the GFC's impact on India can be identified:

(*i*) The financial channel, i.e., the growing integration of India's financial markets with global financial markets;

(*ii*) The growing trade links between India and the rest of the world indicate that exports would decline quite sharply, and;

(*iii*) A final avenue is the confidence channel.

The tightened global liquidity situation following from the failure of Lehman brothers in September 2008 increased the risk-aversion of several banks and other lending institutions. There is a slowdown in India's growth performance-but not a collapse. The short-run outlook for the Indian economy is unclear. Real GDP growth and major sectors have shown strong signs of slipping. But, the stimulus packages announced by the government and the RBI have had their desired effect. The substantial fiscal stimulus provided by Govt of India through supplementary demand for grants has reduced adverse impacts partially. The additional spending on health , education and other infrastructure has revived current demand in India. Assuming that the global economy starts picking up in 2009-10, of which there are some signs, and provided developed countries do not resort to widespread protectionism, an assumption that may be proved wrong, the Indian economy should be in a good position to register a strong comeback.

Though at the current time, the focus of the world is on the developments in the Satyam saga; its impact in the medium to long run will be minimal. Indian outsourcing companies have a definite opportunity before them to become leaders in the segment. To achieve this, companies are going to have to identify new markets and service areas which will enable them to scale up both their geographical presence as well as revenues. The key to achieving preferred vendor status is going to rest upon their ability to create technology and process IPs through collaboration and co-creation with their clients. Finally, to fully enable themselves to compete with companies like IBM and Accenture, Indian companies will have to manage an image makeover which will enable them to transition into global companies headquartered in India. If they are able to achieve these objectives within the next 3-5 years by taking advantage of the current economic conditions, an Indian IT company(s) might become the inheritor to the mantle that is currently being alternated between IBM and HP. To enhance the growth potential of India, the adverse impacts of recession must be mitigated through additional spending and higher credit flow through our banking system.

REFERENCES

Claessens, S., Kose M. A and Terrones M. E. (2008) *Global financial crisis: How long? How deep?*

Islam, M. S. (2008) : South Asia's inflation challenges, *ISAS insights,* No-26, Singapore, 28 March

Lahiri, A. (2009) : *Indian Financial Reforms : National Priorities Amidst An International Crisis.* Sir Purushotamadas Thakurdas Memorial Lecture, Mumbai.

Mathur, B.P. (2009) : Global Economic Crisis : Lessons for India, *Mainstream*, Volume XLVII, No. 25.

Nachane, D.M. (2007) : Liberalization of the Capital Account : Perils and Possible Safeguards. *Economic and Political Weekly*, Vol. XLII, No. 36, Sept. 8-14, pp. 3633-3643.

National Commission for Enterprises in the Unorganized Sector (NCEUS) (Nov. 2008) : The Global Economic Crisis and the Informal Economy in India, Government of India.

Planning Commission, Government of India (2008) : *Eleventh Five Year Plan,* Vol. III.

Rediff.com. news (2008) : *How the global financial crisis affect* India?

Suba Rao, D. (2009) : *The Global Economic Crisis and Challenges for the Asian Economy in a changing World,* Speech delivered at the Symposium, Tokyo 18 February.

Sung hoon Cho (2007) : Financial Institutions and Markets, *Korea's Economic,* Vol. 23.

The Economist (2008) : The Decoupling Debate, 6th March.

United Nations (2009) : *World Economic Situation and Prospects,* New York.

World Bank (2008) : *Global Financial Crisis—Implications for South Asian Regions,* 21st October.

CHAPTER

Global Economic Meltdown and its Impact on India

Rajesh D. Shelke

ABSTRACT

The financial crisis has become a worldwide tsunami that threatens the health of virtually every economy today and is almost on the verge of a recession. The global financial crisis triggered by the fall of financial institutions in the United States is casting its shadow all over the world. The most immediate effect of that crisis on India has been an outflow of foreign institutional investment from the equity market. Foreign institutional investors, who need to retrench assets in order to cover losses in their home countries and are seeking havens of safety in an uncertain environment, have become major sellers in Indian markets. In a response to the developments in the global financial markets, the Reserve Bank of India has announced a series of measures aimed at increasing liquidity and attracting foreign currency. The RBI has also asked the primary dealer not to undertake transactions in government security in the primary market. In conclusion it is difficult to insulate India or any other country from the effects of American problems. The problem arose because of the complexity of the financial products and innovations introduced in the American financial system. Innovation for the sake of innovation can be disastrous. The American experience should be a guide to us to avoid such pitfalls. The current economic recession is indeed very severing. However, its impact on India should be milder, partly because our economy is not as globalised as many others are and are partly because our financial institutions are on sound footing. With proper policy inventions, which are already in place, the country should be able to recover in the next few months.

KEYWORDS

Financial crisis, Liquidity, RBI, Policy inventions

Introduction

The global financial crisis is into its third year now. Many have termed is the "worst financial crisis of the last century". The crisis began in the U.S. and Europe and it has since affected the rest of the world, including Asia, in a bigger way than was thought at the beginning.

"Financial crisis" is a very broad term that covers a whole range of events, including crashes in the housing market, stock market, foreign exchange market, current accounts of nations and, of course, problems afflicting the banking sector. There is evidence that the really severe financial crisis is those in which the banking sector is affected.

The turmoil in the international financial markets of advanced economies, that started around mid-2007 has exacerbated substantially since august 2008. The financial market crisis has led to the collapse of major financial institutions and is now beginning to impact the real economy in the advanced economies. As this crisis is unfolding, credit markets appear to be drying up in the developed world.

Financial crisis in the market economies of democratic countries is not unusual it is also not unusual for such economies to make policy correction and come out of the crisis. During this first decade of the 21st century itself we have seen economies in the west go through two crisis: The first was in 2000, the "dotcom. bust" and the second was after the 9/11 terror attacks. But the market economies came out of it.

In fact we saw a boom between 2003 to 2008. But in the recent time, the world economy is facing the financial crisis.

The financial crisis has become a worldwide tsunami that threatens the health of virtually every economy today and is almost on the verge of a recession. The global financial crisis triggered by the fall of financial institutions in the United States is casting its shadow all over the world.

As the financial turmoil countries to better world economies, triggering the collapse of more number of financial and other institutions, the bailout packages from different Governments globally announced. The IMF progress report released has said that no country could escape global turmoil fully and that India would face a slowdown in its growth rate. Financial crisis can have a severe effect on economies. This is well known. What is not so well recognised is that the severity of the impact can vary widely.

The IMF (2008) notes that "financial stress episodes are more likely to be followed be severe economic downturns when they occur in the context of a rapid build-up in credit and house prices and a heavier reliance on credit by firms and households". In other words, the greater the imbalances and excesses, the greater the fall.

Severity of the Present Crisis

In the paper by Reinhert and Rogoff (2008b) focus on 18 major post-war banking crisis in the developed world and three in emerging markets. They arrive at the following conclusions :

1. Real housing prices decline by an average of 36 per cent over five years and equity prices by 56 per cent over three and a half years.
2. The unemployment rate rises by 7 percentage points on the average over a period of four years while output falls from peak-to-trough by 9 per cent over a shorter period, two years.

3. The real value of government debt tends to explode, rising by an average of 86 per cent in the major post-second world war episodes.

It would be incorrect, therefore to see the present crisis of the global economy as something that flows inexorably from the imbalances created in the past several years. Two points are worth emphasizing. First while a correction was overdue, it need not have been as severe as it is turning out to be if the financial system had been regulated, if we were to put together all the adverse factors in the economic environment-current account imbalances, greedy bankers, excess reserves of Asian economies, low interest rates housing bubbles and sub-prime loans - it does not follow that these must translate into a global financial crisis. Secondly it is also arguable that the economic impact could have been better contained had the policy response been better. The broader point is that we cannot afford to take a mechanistic view of financial crisis and their economic impact going by averages estimated from the past. The quality of policy response can make a world of difference.

Impact of the Crisis on India

The most immediate effect of that crisis on India has been an outflow of foreign institutional investment from the equity market. Foreign institutional investors, who need to retrench assets in order to cover losses in their home countries and are seeking havens of safety in an uncertain environment, have become major sellers in Indian markets.

The result has been the observed sharp depreciation of the rupee. While this depreciation may be good for India's exports that are adversely affected by the slowdown in global markets, it is not good for those who have accumulated foreign exchange payment commitments. Not does it assist the government's effort to rein in inflation. A second route through which the global financial crisis could affect India is through the exposure of Indian banks or bank operating in India to the impaired assets resulting from the sub-prime crisis.

Finally the recession generated by the financial crisis in the advanced economies as a group and the US in particular, will adversely affect India's exports, especially its exports of software and IT - enabled services, more than 60 per cent of which are directed to the U.S.

International banks and financial institutions in the US and EU are important sources of demand for such services, and the difficulties they face will result in some curtailment of their demand. Further the nationalisation of many of these banks is likely to increase the pressure to reduce outsourcing in order to keep jobs in the developed countries.

And the slowing of growth outside of the financial sector too will have implication for both merchandise and service exports. The net result would be a smaller export stimulus and widening trade deficit.

Impact on Agriculture

The global financial crisis has cast its indirect impact on our agricultural sector, especially on cash crops such as cotton, coffee and sugarcane as detailed below:

Stagnation in Cotton Production and Consumption

1. The area under cotton during 2008-09 is expected to be only 92.6 lakh hectares as against 95.55 lakh hectares during the previous season.
2. The production in 2007-08 was 315 lakh bales of cotton and exports alone were 85 lakh bales in 2007-08.However due to global financial crisis and the low international demand, the exports were expected to decline to 75 lakh bales this year.
3. Use of cotton by world mills has been expected to decline by one per cent in 2008-09, i.e. 26.2 million tonnes due to slower global economic growth and higher prices of cotton related to polyster.

4. The domestic consumption of cotton is also expected to remain the same during this year as at 226 lakh bales in 2007-08, though it was estimated at 322 lakh bales for the year earlier.

However, added to the slower pace of global economic growth and higher prices of cotton is the main reason for reduction in cotton trade.

Tumbling Down of Coffee Prices

1. Coffee prices in the International market have tumbled due to the global meltdown.
2. The entry of substantial volumes of coffee from good harvest in Brazil and Vietnam hads dampened the prices further.
3. In India, 70 per cent of the coffee output is exported and this heavy dependence on exports has posed a threat to jobs in coffee plantations.

The global crisis would continue to dog the world, depending on how the Governments act. However the Indian economy has the resilience and capability to face the global crisis and circumvent the shadow cast on the agricultural scenario.

Impact of US Recession on Indian Economy

The following sectors are mostly affected by the present US recession.

Impact on Portfolio Investment Inflows

According to Prime Minister's Economic Advisory Council chairman Mr. Suresh Tendulkar, Economic environment has become uncertain, portfolio investment (in India) will be adversely affected. The major impact, he said, will be on funding of infrastructure sector projects, as it will become difficult for domestic companies to garner overseas funds in adequate quantities. The present financial crisis in U.S.A.

definitely would affect the portfolio investment inflows in India.

Impact on IT Sector

The Indian IT Industry, already reeling under the impact of US credit crisis as customers hold back their IT spends, earns about a third of its revenues from the financial services sector and the latest development could prolong the impact.

Impact on Employment

According to the experts the job loss due to the current crisis could be anywhere between 15,000 and 25,000 people in the Indian IT Industry over the next six months in Indian and abroad.

Impact on Tourism Sector

Travel industry experts told that the inbound tourism in India will slump by 20 to 30 per cent compared to last year. This downturn might negatively impact the hotel bookings and occupations as well. If the US stays under this financial crisis for long, it is going to have a negative impact on hotel industry in India.

Impact on Rupees and Bonds

As news of bankruptcy of major ventures in U.S.A. the rupee breached the highest level against the dollar. Widening arbitrage in the overseas non-deliverable forwards (NDF) market and weakening of other major currencies such as the euro and pound against dollar dragged down the rupee sharply.

Impact on Real Estate Market

Indian property prices, which had taken off like jet planes, appear to be losing altitude after bad debts owing their origin to real estate brought down by the US financial market to its knees. The experts told that the current environment was challenging to the Indian real estate market and there could be some decline in prices due to the negative sentiment. The slowdown is also because of high interest rate regime.

Impact on Recruitment

A student placement representative holds that there has been no official intimation as yet from the investment bankers regarding the recruitment as this sector is also facing severe impacts of US recession.

Impact on Commodities Market

Most agricultural commodities ended the season in the red on the domestic developments.

Measures by RBI to ease Pressure on Market

In a response to the developments in the global financial markets, the Reserve Bank of India has announced a series of measures aimed at increasing liquidity and attracting foreign currency. The RBI has also asked the primary dealer not to undertake transactions in government security in the primary market.

Reasons of Recession

To understand how this crisis originated in the U.S. and spread across all countries in the globe, we need to understand the inter-linkage of the countries in the globalisation of process. These linkages are through three channels, the financial sector, export and exchange rate. The crisis in the credit market subsequently spread to the real/commodity as well. But how did it affect the real/commodity market? In fact, once the credit market gets dented, the whole chain of money supply got adversely affected. At one level there was liquidity crunch as the financial institutions held toxic assets and nobody wanted to lose whatever liquidity they had. They did not allow whatever liquid assets they had for lending because they lost faith in the whole system. With credit crunch, commodity sector got hurt, investment plans were put on hold and business confidence was shaken. The commodity market was also affected because with the collapse of the financial institutions, people lost their jobs and commodity demand slumped. Subsequently, commodity prices sunk and inventory piled up. The result has been a global meltdown of huge magnitude.

Conclusions

The world is in the midst of a severe financial crisis, meaning a crisis that will exact a huge cost in terms of lost economic growth. It is not true; however, that all financial crisis are severe. There is a high probability of a financial crisis having an impact on the real economy when there is disruption of the banking sector. Second the severity of the crisis is not independent of the policy response. An appropriate policy response does help contain the depth and period of an economic downturn.

In the present crisis we contend that the decision to let Lehman Brothers fail was an important landmark. Until then, it was reasonable to expect that the downturn in the U.S. economy would not be very deep and prolonged and the impact on the global economy too would not be great. This is what most forecasts until the Lehman episode had us believe. The revision in forecasts thereafter was occasioned by the consequences of the Lehman failure, especially the loss of confidence among money market funds and the rise in premier on credit default swaps, both of which had serious repercussions for a whole range of financial institutions.

India will not escape unscathed in the present crisis because its economy has become more integrated with the rest of the world over the past decade and a half. Overseas finance has become increasingly important for Indian corporate and the drying up of such finance is bound to tell on their fortunes. There is also a broader impact arising from tighter liquidity conditions and a decline in stock prices. India's authorities have responded to the crisis with both fiscal and monetary stimuli although the scope for the former appears somewhat limited given India's fiscal position. The Indian banking sector is well placed to weather the storm because it is not directly exposed to the financial crisis. It faces secondary effects arising from the slowdown of the economy.

REFERENCES

"Recession definition". Business Dictionary.com. 2007–2008. Retrieved 19 November 2008.

Business Cycle Expansions and Contractions". National Bureau of Economic Research. Retrieved 19 November 2008.

Siegel, Jeremy J. (2002). Stocks for the Long Run: The Definitive Guide to Financial Market Returns and Long-Term Investment Strategies, 3rd, New York: McGraw-Hill, 388.

Fragile economy improves but not out of woods yet: Financial News.

2003 Business Cycle Dating Committee, July 2003, National Bureau of Economic Research.

Reinhert, Carmen and Kenneth Rogoff (2008b) "The Aftermath of Financial Crisis", paper prepared for presentation at the American Economic Association, 3 January 2009.

CHAPTER

Global Financial Crisis and its Impact on Indian Economy

Dr. A. Abdul Raheem
Dr. Abdus Shukur
Dr. M. Abdul Jamal

INTRODUCTION

The term 'Financial Crisis' is applied broadly to a variety of situations in which some financial institutions or assets suddenly lose a large part of their value. The 19th and 20th centuries witnessed many kinds of financial crisis such as banking panics, recessions stock market crashes, currency crisis, sovereign defaults and so on. Many economists have offered theories about how financial crises develop and how they could be prevented. There is little consensus, however, and financial crisis are still a regular occurrence around the World.

FINANCIAL CRISIS : A BACKGROUND

The sub prime mortgage crisis triggered by a dramatic rise in mortgage delinquencies and foreclosures in United States had a major adverse effect on financial markets and banks. The crisis, which has its roots in the closing years of the 20th century, became apparent in 2007 and has exposed pervasive weaknesses in financial industry regulation and the global financial system. The main reasons for the present financial crisis are as follows:

- Boom and burst in the housing market.
- Speculation.
- High risk mortgage loans lending/borrowing practices.
- Securitization practices.
- Inaccurate credit ratings.
- Government polices.
- Polices of central bank.
- Financial institutions debt level and incentives.
- Credit default swaps.

In its "Declaration of the Summit on Financial Markets and the World Economy," dated 15th November 2008, leaders of the Group 20 cited the following causes:

(*a*) Inadequate appreciation of the risks and failure to exercise proper due diligence.

(*b*) Weak underwriting standards, unsound risk management practices, increasingly complex and opaque financial products, and consequent excessive leverage combined to create vulnerabilities in the system.

(*c*) Policy-makers, regulators and supervisors, of some advanced countries, did not adequately appreciate and address the risks building up in financial markets, keep pace with financial innovation, or consider the systematic ramifications of domestic regulatory actions.

GLOBAL FINANCIAL CRISIS AND INDIA

India like most other emerging economies has so far not been seriously affected by the financial turmoil. The relative freedom from the contagion spreading from the global tsunami on the Indian financial system owes much to the wise and judicious policies of our central bank and the government of India. Besides it is very much needed to ensure that India remains an island of stability. At a time when the total deregulation was the order of the day in 90s, Dr. Manmohan Singh as the Finance Minister authorized a path breaking study of the Indian financial system by experienced central banker, M. Narasimhan.

Government of India and RBI accepted the recommendations of Narasimhan Committee Report and proceeded to implement them. India did not go for the segregation of investment and commercial banking. The Indian banking system is basically owed by public sector. There is greater confidence of depositors in a state owned bank than in a privately owned bank. Besides India avoided the temptation of full capital account convertibility which saved in India from the catastrophic mess of financial crisis. The stabilizing role played by securities and exchange board of India needs special appreciation with regard to the regulation of various financial instruments especially in the case of participatory notes.

The Reserve Bank of India had put in place steps to mitigate liquidity risks at the short-end, risk at the systemic level and at the institution level as well. Some of the important measures by the Reserve Bank of India in this regard include, first restriction the over night unsecured market for funds to banks and primary dealers as well as limits on the borrowing and lending operations of these entities in the over night inter-bank call money market. Large reliance by banks on borrowed funds can exacerbate vulnerability to external shocks. This has been brought out quite strikingly in the ongoing financial crisis in the global financial markets. The assets liability management guidelines for dealing with overall asset-liability mismatches take into account both on and off balance sheet items. Finally guidelines on securitization of standard assets have laid down a detailed policy on provision of liquidity support to special purpose vehicles.

IMPACT OF THE CRISIS ON INDIA

While the overall policy approach has been able to mitigate the potential impact of the turmoil on domestic financial markets and the economy, with the increasing integration of the Indian economy and its financial markets with rest of the world, there is recognition that the country does face some downside risks from these international developments. The risks arise mainly from the potential reversal of capital flows on a sustained medium-term basis from the projected slow down of the global economy, particularly in advanced economies, and from some elements of potential financial contagion. In India, the adverse effects have so far been mainly in the equity markets because of reversal of portfolio equity flows, and the concomitant effects on the domestic forex market and liquidity conditions. The macro effects have so far been muted due to the overall strength of domestic demand, the healthy balance sheets of the Indian corporate sector, and the predominant domestic financing of investment.

Table 4.1. Impact of the Crisis on India

(US $ million)

	2007-08	2008-09
Component		
Foreign Direct Investment to India	8,536	16,733
External Commercial Borrowings (net)	6,990	1,559
Short-term Trade Credits (net)	1,804	2,173
Memo		
ECB Approvals	13,375	8,127
Foreign Exchange Reserves (variation)	48,583	–17,904
Foreign Exchange Reserves (end-period)	247,762	291,819

As might be expected, the main impact of the global financial turmoil in India has emanated from the significant change experienced in the capital account in 2008-09 so far, relative to the previous year (Table 4.1). Total net capital flows fell from US$17.3 billion in April-June 2007 to US$13.2 billion in April-June 2008. Nonetheless, capital flows are expected to be more than sufficient to cover the current account deficit this year as well. While Foreign Direct Investment (FDI) inflows have continued to exhibit accelerated growth (US$ 16.7 billion during April-August 2008 as compared with US$ 8.5 billion in the corresponding period of 2007), portfolio investments by foreign institutional investors (FIIs) witnessed a net outflow of about US$ 6.4 billion in April-September 2008 as compared with a net inflow of US$ 15.5 billion in the corresponding period last year.

Similarly, external commercial borrowings of the corporate sector declined from US$ 7.0 billion in April-June 2007 to US$ 1.6 billion in April-June 2008, partially in response to policy measures in the face of excess flows in 2007-08, but also due to the current turmoil in advanced economies. With the existence of a merchandise trade deficit of 7.7 per cent of GDP in 2007-08, and a current account deficit of 1.5 per cent, and change in perceptions with respect to capital flows, there has been significant pressure on the Indian exchange rate in recent months. Whereas the real exchange rate appreciated from an index of 104.9 (base 1993-94=100) (US$1 = Rs. 46.12) in September 2006 to 115.0 (US$ 1 = Rs. 40.34) in September 2007, it has now depreciated to a level of 101.5 (US $ 1 = Rs. 48.74) as on October 8, 2008.

IMPACT ON THE INDIAN BANKING SYSTEM

One of the key features of the current financial turmoil has been the lack of perceived contagion being felt by banking systems in EMEs, particularly in Asia. The Indian banking system also has not experienced any contagion, similar to its peers in the rest of Asia. A detailed study undertaken by the RBI in September 2007 on the impact of the subprime episode on the Indian banks had revealed that none of the Indian banks or the foreign banks, with whom the discussions had been held, had any direct exposure to the sub-prime markets in the U.S.A. or other markets. However, a few Indian banks had invested in the collateralised debt obligations (CDOs) / bonds which had a few underlying entities with sub-prime exposures. Thus, no direct impact on account of direct exposure to the sub-prime market was in evidence. However, a few of these banks did suffer some losses on account of the mark-to-market losses caused by the widening of the credit spreads arising from the sub-prime episode on term liquidity in the market, even though the overnight markets remained stable.

Consequent upon filling of bankruptcy under Chapter 11 by Lehman Brothers, all banks were advised to report the details of their exposures to Lehman Brothers and related entities both in India and abroad. Out of 77 reporting banks, 14 reported exposures to Lehman Brothers and its related entities either in India or abroad. An analysis of the information reported by these banks revealed that majority of the exposures reported by the banks pertained to subsidiaries of Lehman Bros Holdings Inc. which are not covered by the bankruptcy proceedings. Overall, these banks' exposure especially to Lehman Brothers Holding Inc. which has filed for bankruptcy is not significant and banks are reported to have made adequate provisions.

In the aftermath of the turmoil caused by bankruptcy, the Reserve Bank of India has announced a series of measures to facilitate orderly operation of financial markets and to ensure financial stability which predominantly includes extension of additional liquidity support to banks.

IMPACT ON INDIAN ECONOMY

The current financial crisis would affect India in the following possible ways:

There could be finical contagion and spillovers for stock market: in line with the falling capital markets across the world, which have already wiped out investor wealth of over $ 10 trillion this year so far, the Indian stock market has witnessed an unprecedented fall over the past few months. Not surprisingly, FII have been pulling out from the stock market in a big way, corporate borrowings from the global markets are becoming increasingly difficult, raising money for new investments through public issues is on hold, and liquidity in the economy is f drying up. The most immediate effect of the crisis on India has been an outflow of foreign institutional investment from the equity market. Foreign institutional investors, who need to retrench assets in order to cover losses in their home countries and are seeking havens of safety in an uncertain environment, have become major sellers in Indian markets.

In 2007-08, net FII inflows into India amounted to $20.3 billion. As compared with this, they pulled out $11.1 billion during the first nine-and-a-half months of calendar year 2008, of which $ 8.3 billion occurred over the first six-and-a-half months of financial year 2008-09 (April 1 to October 16).

Given the importance of FII investment in driving Indian stock markets and the fact that cumulative investments by FII stood at $ 66.5 billion at the beginning of this calendar year, the pullout triggered a collapse in stock prices. As a result, the sensex fell from its closing peak of 20,873 on January 8, 2008, to less than 10,000 by October 17, 2008.

Falling Rupee

In addition, this withdrawal by the FIIs led to a sharp depreciation of the rupee. Between January 1 and October 16, 2008, the RBI reference rate for the rupee fell by nearly 25 per cent, even relative to a weak currency like the dollar, from Rs. 39.20 to the dollar to Rs. 48.86. This was despite the sale of dollar by the RBI, which was reflected in a decline of $ 25.8 billion in its foreign currency assets between the end of March 2008 and October 3, 2008.

It could be argued that the $ 275 billion the RBI still has in its kitty is adequate to stall and reverse any further depreciation if needed. But given the sudden exit by the FIIs, the RBI is clearly not keen to deplete its reserves too fast and risk a foreign exchange crisis. The result has been the observed sharp depreciation of the rupee. While this depreciation may be good for India's exports that are adversely affected by the slowdown in global markets, it is not so good for those who have accumulated foreign exchange payment commitments. Nor dose it assist the Government's effort to rein in inflation.

Exposure of Banks

So far the RBI has claimed that the exposure of Indian banks to assets impaired by the financial crisis in small. According to reports, the RBI had estimated that as a result of exposure to collateralized debt obligations and credit default swaps, the combined mark-to-market losses of Indian banks at the end of July was around $ 450 million. Given the aggressive strategies adopted by the private sector banks, the MTM losses incurred by public sectors banks were estimated at $ 90 million, while that for private banks around $ 360 million. As yet these losses are on paper, but the RBI believes that even if they are to be provided for, these banks are well capitalised and can easily take the hit.

Such assurances have neither reduced fears of those exposed to these banks or to investors holding shares in these banks. These fears are compounded by those of the minority in metropolitan areas dealing with foreign banks that have expanded their presence in India, whose global exposure to toxic assets must be substantial. What is disconcerting is the limited information available on the risks to which depositors and investors are subject. Only time will tell how significant this factor will be in making India vulnerable to the global crisis.

Losses Sustained by Non-banking Financial Institutions

The indirect fallout of the global crisis and its ripples in India is in the form of the losses sustained by non-bank financial institutions (especially mutual funds) and corporate firms, as a result of their exposure to domestic stock currency markets. Such losses are expected to be large, as signed by the decision of the RBI to allow banks to provide loans to mutual funds against certificates of deposit (CDs) or buyback their own CDs before maturity. These losses are bound to render some institutions fragile, with implications that would become clear only in the coming months.

India's Export

The recession generated by the financial crisis in the advanced economies as a group and the U.S. in particular, will adversely affect India's exports, especially its exports of software and IT-enabled services, more than 60 per cent of which are directed to the U.S. International banks and financial institutions in the U.S. and E.U. are important sources of demand for such services, and the difficulties they face will result in some curtailment of their demand. Further, the nationalization of many of these banks is likely to increase the pressure to reduce outsourcing in order to keep jobs in t counties. And the slowing of growth outside of the financial sector too will have implications for both merchandise and services exports. The net result would be a smaller export stimulus and a widening trade deficit.

Trade Deficit Surges to $ 49.1 Billion during April-August

Latest provisional figures released by the Commerce Ministry shows that the country's exports during August 2008 at $ 16 billion were 26.9 per cent higher than level of $ 12.6 billion during August 2007, while cumulatively exports during the first five months of the current fiscal at $ 81.2 billion were

35.1 per cent higher than the level of $ 60.1 billion in the corresponding period of last fiscal. In rupee terms, exports at Rs. 3.42 lakh crore during April-August 2008 grew by 39.1 per cent from Rs. 2.46 lakh crore in the corresponding months of the previous fiscal.

Table 4.2. Trade Deficit durint April-August 2007-2008

(in $ billion)

	August			April-August		
	2008	2007	% Growth	2008-09	2007-08	% Growth
Exports	16	12.6	26.9	81.2	60.1	35.1
Imports	29.9	19.8	51.2	130.3	94.6	37.7
Oil Imports	10.96	6.2	76.7	45.96	28.8	59.6

On the import front, imports during August at $ 29.9 billion showed a hefty 51.2 per cent growth against $ 19.8 billion in August 2007, while cumulatively imports during the period under review at $ 130.3 billion grew by 37.7 per cent over the level of $ 94.6 billion during April – August 2008 at Rs 5.50 lakh crore against Rs 3.87 lakh crore in the comparable months of the previous fiscal (Table 4.2).

Oil Imports

Oil imports during August 2008 at $ 10.96 billion were 76.7 per cent higher than oil imports of $ 6.2 billion in the corresponding months of 2007, while cumulative oil imports at $ 45.96 billion were 59.6 per cent higher than the oil imports of $ 28.8 billion in the corresponding period last year. Non-oil imports in August 2008 at $ 18.9 billion were 39.6 per cent higher than such imports of $ 13.6 billion in August 2007, while cumulative non-oil imports during the period under review at $ 84.4 billion (Table 4.2). Commerce Ministry officials say that while export growth was buoyed up by the depreciating rupee and also supplemented by high growth in traditional items such as engineering goods, chemicals and non-traditional items such as petroleum product exports, they are worried over the sustainability of this uninterrupted uptrend particularly after November 2008 when the effects of the financial market turmoil and slowdown in import demand from major markets such as the US and Europe would start playing themselves out.

Lower Growth Projections

It is a well known fact that there will be lower growth rates as compared to the previous years for India in the midst of global economic melt down.

The Asian Development Bank (ADB) down- scaled the growth expectations of many Asian economies, including India's in its half yearly report: Asian Development Outlook 2008. The ADB attributes this to the worsening conditions in major industrial economies that will weaken demand for goods and services. "The myth of uncoupling has been exploded", the report says. India's GDP gro3wth estimate for the current fiscal (2008-09) has been downgraded from 8 per cent to 7.4 per cent and, for the next financial year (2009-10), from 8.5 per cent to 7 per cent.

KEYS ISSUES TO BE ADDRESSED

The key issues to be addressed in the present scenario are as follows :

- Domestic liquidity shortage.
- Exchange rate volatility and reduction in access to foreign currency funds.
- Inadequate credit availability and slowdown in demand.
- Decline in business and investor confidence and optimism.

CONCLUSION

India has by and large been spared of global financial contagion due to the supreme turmoil for a variety of reasons.

India's growth process has been largely domestic demand driven and its reliance on foreign savings gas remained around 1.5 per cent in recent period. It also has a very comfortable level of forex reserves. The credit derivatives market is in an embryonic stage; there are restrictions on investments by residents in such products issued abroad; and regularly guidelines on securitization do not permit immediate profit recognition. Financial stability in India has been achieved through perseverance of prudential policies which prevent institutions from excessive risk taking, and financial markets from becoming extremely volatile and turbulent.

REFERENCES

"Global Financial Crisis and key risks: impact on India and Asia", Remarks prepared for IMF-FSF-Rakeash Mohan, Deputy Governor, Reserve Bank of India.

"Declaration of the summit on Financial markets and the World economy", November 2008.

"Global Financial Crisis : reflections on itsimpact on India", *Business Line*, November 2008.

"Global financial crisis anddevelopingcountries", A background note-overseases Development institute.

"Dealing with the impact of global financial crisis",an eleven point agenda - Confederation of Indian industries.

Henry, Peter Blair (2007), "Capital Account Liberalization: Theory, Evidence, and Speculation", *Journal of Economic Literature*, Vol. XLV, December.

Mohan, Rakesh (2006), "Coping With Liquidity Management in India: A Practitioner's View", *Reserve Bank of India Bulletin*, April.

Prasad, Eswar S., Raghuram G. Rajan and Arvind Subramanian (2007), "Foreign Capital and Economic Growth", *Brookings Papers on Economic Activity*, 1.

Reserve Bank of India (2008), *Annual Policy Statement for the Year 2008-09*, April.

CHAPTER

Indian Economy in the Midst of Global Financial Meltdown

Aditya Kumar Patra

The global financial crisis of 2008 has been termed by many as the worst financial crisis, a second Great Depression. The beginning of the crisis, triggered by US sub-prime crisis, can be traced back to August 2007. The run on the Northern Rock, the U.K. mortgage bank, in mid-September 2007, the Wall Street Crash in November 2007 and the merger of Bear Sterns with JP Morgan in mid-March 2008 are some of the important events in the building up of the crisis. However, the crisis becomes culminated with the collapse of the Lehman Brothers in mid-September 2008.

For more than a year since the outbreak of the crisis, the leaders and economists in emerging market economies assured their citizens as well as foreign investors that their financial systems were safely insulated from that of the western economies. Hence, free from any fear of crisis. The basis of this robust optimism was the 'Decoupling Hypothesis' which was endorsed by *The Economist*. The decoupling hypothesis stands on the following axioms.

(1) Trade linkages of emerging economies with the US had diminished and trade linkage among emerging markets had become more important than in the past.

(2) Growth of leading emerging markets was mainly driven by domestic demand.

(3) Over the past decades, the emerging markets had adopted several economic reforms, as a result of which they had become more stable and efficient.

Therefore, the Asian economies, especially ASEAN-5, China and India would not only remain insulated from the crisis but also play a pivotal role in moderating the global downturn and paving the way for a worldwide recovery with in a short span of time.

It was the fall of Lehman Brothers in September 2008 had changed the situation dramatically. As *The Economist*, London observed in October 2008, "It is not only the geographical breadth of the crisis that it is alarming but also its economic depth". The global meltdown was American in origin and is spread in two directions-geographically across Atlantic from the U.S. to Europe and sectorally from financial markets to the real economy.

India like other emerging markets has suffered a severe impact than supposed earlier. As Reserve Bank of India (RBI) Governor D. Subbarao (2009) has pointed out, it arises from three channels: the trade channel, the financial channel and the confidence channel. Up to the Lehman episode it was assumed that the impact on India would be primarily through the trade channel. For India, this impact would be modest, since merchandise exports accounts for less than 15% of gross domestic product (GDP). But once we factor in the financial channel, the picture changes a lot. As the ratio of external transactions to gross domestic product has been more than doubled from 46.8 per cent in 1997-98 to 117.4 per cent in 2007-08. In a time of global economic crisis, a higher level of financial integration impacts on the economy in three ways: reducing Indian companies' access to overseas finance, lowering domestic liquidity and a fall of stock prices. In a time of global crisis the consumers and investors are having pessimistic attitude. They (employees) generally cut back their spending with a fear to loose their job. Further, banks are either averse to lending altogether or will lend only at a steep interest. The following paragraph depicts the stages through which the global financial crisis spread to India.

Tracking the Spread of Financial Crisis

Stage I : The reversal of capital flows started in January 2008 through a massive disinvestment by foreign institutional investors (FII) from India's equity markets which led to a crash in stock markets. There had been a net FII disinvestment of US$13.3 billion from January 2008 to February 2009 (14 months) in contrast to a net investment of US$17.7 billion during 2007 (12 months).

Stage II : There was a massive slowdown in external commercial borrowing by India's companies, trade credit and banking inflows from April 2008. Short-term trade finance and bank borrowings from abroad swung to outflows of US$9.5 billion and US$11.4 billion respectively in the second half of 2008-09.

Stage III : The crisis struck the foreign exchange markets by May 2008 and the rupee fell by about 20 per cent from May to November 2008. The Reserve Bank of India intervened heavily to support the rupee by selling dollars, leading to some depletion of the stock of reserves. In 2008-09 there was a depletion of India's foreign reserves of US$57.7 billion.

Stage IV : By mid-September 2008, the crisis gripped India's money market. The drying up of funds in the foreign credit markets led to a virtual cessation of external commercial borrowing for India, including the access to short-term trade finance. The collapse of the stock market ruled out the possibility of companies raising funds from the domestic stock market. Indian banks also lost access to funds from abroad, as inter-bank borrowing seized up in the US and Europe and banks had to send funds to their branches abroad in those countries. All these put heavy pressure on domestic banks, leading to a liquidity crisis from mid-September to end-October 2008. This was reflected in the inter-bank call money markets where the call money rates rose to 20 per cent or so.

Stage V : From September 2008, the trade sector collapsed. In the second half of 2008-09, merchandise exports declined by 18 per cent against a growth of 35 per cent in the first half and imports fell by 11 per cent against a growth of 45 per cent in the first half. The growth in software exports dropped to less than four per cent in the second half of 2008-09 (38 per cent growth in the first half) and remittances declined in absolute terms by about 20 per cent in the second half as against a growth of 41 per cent in the first half of 2008-09. Domestic banks responded to the sudden loss of different avenues of funds for the Indian commercial sector and increased their lending during the period of "credit crunch". In September and October 2008, bank finance (non-food credit and investments in shares, bonds, debentures, commercial paper, etc.) expanded more than the previous year, partly compensating for the drying up of funds from other sources.

Stage VI : The crisis spread to the domestic credit market. The real economy deteriorated from September 2008, shown first by the sharp fall in export growth to 10 per cent in that month from about 35 per cent during April-August 2008, and negative growth thereafter; virtually negligible or negative growth in industrial output from October 2008; and negative growth in central tax revenue collection, also from October 2008. Business and consumer confidence began to ebb leading to a decline in overall demand. By November 2008, the situation had fundamentally transformed. Expansion of bank finance to the commercial sector slumped to Rs.609 billion during the four-month period, November 2008 to February 2009, just about a quarter in comparison with the expansion of Rs.2362 billion during the same period a year ago. This was primarily due to a sharp fall in demand for funds as investment and consumption dropped. It was also partly due to banks becoming extremely risk averse with the perception of default rising considerably.

Impact on GDP Growth

The impact of financial crisis on gross domestic product and its components of Indian economy are documented in Table 5.1 and Fig. 5.1. The growth in GDP dropped to 5.8 per cent (year-on-year) during the second half of 2008-09 from 7.8 per cent in the first half. Growth improved slightly to 7.9 per cent in the second quarter of 2009-10. Industry, and particularly the manufacturing sector, was the most severely affected by the crisis. Industrial growth plunged to 1.9 per cent in the second half of 2008-09 from 6.1 per cent in the first half and manufacturing growth collapsed to -0.3 per cent in the second half from 5.3 per cent in the first half. Industrial growth picked up to 8.3 per cent in the second quarter of 2009-10 and manufacturing to 9.2 per cent. The services sector as a whole had been resilient up to the third quarter of 2008-09 but later showed signs of weakness with its growth declining to 8.6 per cent in the last quarter of 2008-09 (average 10 per cent growth in the previous three quarters) and picked up to 9.3 per cent in the second quarter of 2009-10.

Policy Measures

To counter-act the menace of financial crisis Government of India has adopted an expansionary monetary policy and contra-cyclical fiscal stimulus packages.

Monetary Policy Responses

Prior to Lehman collapse RBI was engaged in fighting inflation. Inflation measured in terms of the Wholesale Price Index (WPI) peaked at 12.9 per cent in early August 2008. to keep the rising prices under control RBI adopted tight monetary policy. However, RBI's policy response has been changed since October 2008. the RBI acted aggressively from mid-October to ease the situation by a series of rate cutting and liquidity injecting measures that went on till April 2009. The principal monetary responses since October 2008 include:

Table 5.1. Y-o-Y Growth Rate of India's GDP and its components (2006-7 to 2009-10)

Year	Agriculture	Industry	Services	Total
2006-07	**3.8**	**11.0 (12.0)**	**11.2**	**9.6**
Q1	2.7	10.0 (11.7)	11.6	9.6
Q2	3.2	10.7 (12.2)	11.5	10.1
Q3	4.0	10.3 (11.3)	11.1	9.3
Q4	4.9	11.4 (12.8)	10.6	9.7
2007-08	**4.9**	**8.1 (8.2)**	**10.9**	**9.0**
Q1	4.3	9.2 (10.0)	10.8	9.2
Q2	3.9	9.1 (8.2)	10.3	9.0
Q3	8.1	8.2 (8.6)	10.3	9.3
Q4	2.2	6.7 (6.3)	11.8	8.6
2008-09	**1.6**	**3.9 (2.4)**	**9.7**	**6.7**
Q1	3.0	6.0 (5.5)	10.2	7.8
Q2	2.7	6.1 (5.1)	9.8	7.7
Q3	-0.8	2.3 (0.9)	10.2	5.8
Q4	2.7	1.4 (-1.4)	8.6	5.8
2009-10	**0.2**	**8.3**	**7.8**	**6.7**
Q1	2.4	5.0 (3.4)	7.8	6.1
Q2	0.9	8.3 (9.2)	9.3	7.9
Q3	-2.8	11.6 (14.3)	6.3	6.0

Note: Figures in parantheses are percentage growth of manufacturing sector.
Source: CSO.

1. Reduction in the Repo Rate (RR) from nine per cent to 4.75 per cent.
2. Reduction in the reverse Repo Rate from six per cent to 3.25 per cent.
3. Reduction in the Cash Reserve Ratio (CRR) from nine per cent to five per cent.

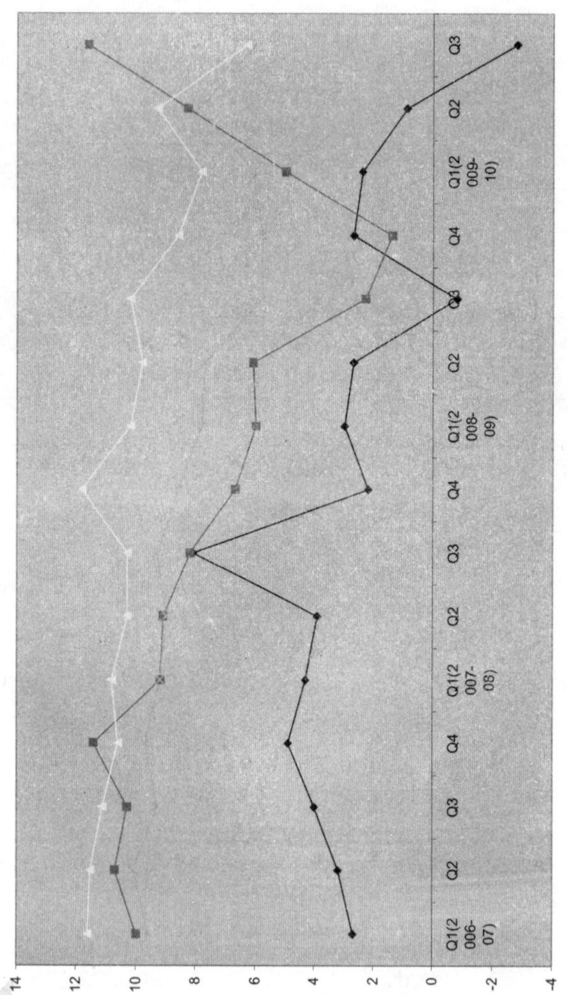

Fig. 5.1. Y-o-Y Growth of GDP and its components in India

4. Reduction in the Statutory Liquidity Ratio (SLR) from 25 per cent to 24 per cent.

In addition to the above mentioned rate cuts RBI adopted several other measures to support liquidity. These include special windows for banks to lend to mutual funds, Non-Banking Financial Companies (NBFCs) and housing finance companies. The central bank also opened refinance facilities for banks, the Small Industrial Development Banks (SIDBI), the National Housing Banks (NHB), and the EXIM Bank besides introducing a liquidity facility for NBFCs through a Special Purpose Vehicle (SPV), and increasing export credit refinance. The RBI also made dollar swap arrangements for branches of Indian banks in the US and Europe facing shortage of dollar funds with the seizing up of the inter-bank markets there.

Fiscal Policy Responses

The Centre had put in place three fiscal stimulus packages in quick succession: December 2008, January 2009 and February 2009. An across-the-board central excise duty reduction by 4 percentage points in December 2008 foregoing revenue to the exchequer to the extent of Rs. 31000 crs. Further, a two per cent reduction in excise duty and service tax and extension of previous excise cut beyond March 2009, announced in February 2009 costing the exchequer Rs. 29,100 crores. Steps taken under recapitalization of banks (in January 2009) include increasing credit availability by additional capital infusion in Scheduled Commercial Banks to the extent of Rs. 20000 crores and providing greater access to market borrowings for State Governments and Indian Infrastructure Financing Company to the extent of Rs. 71000 crores.

The total fiscal burden for these packages amounted to 1.8 per cent of GDP. The central budget 2008-09 announced in February 2008 showed a low fiscal deficit of 2.5 per cent of GDP. But the actual deficit turned out to be much higher

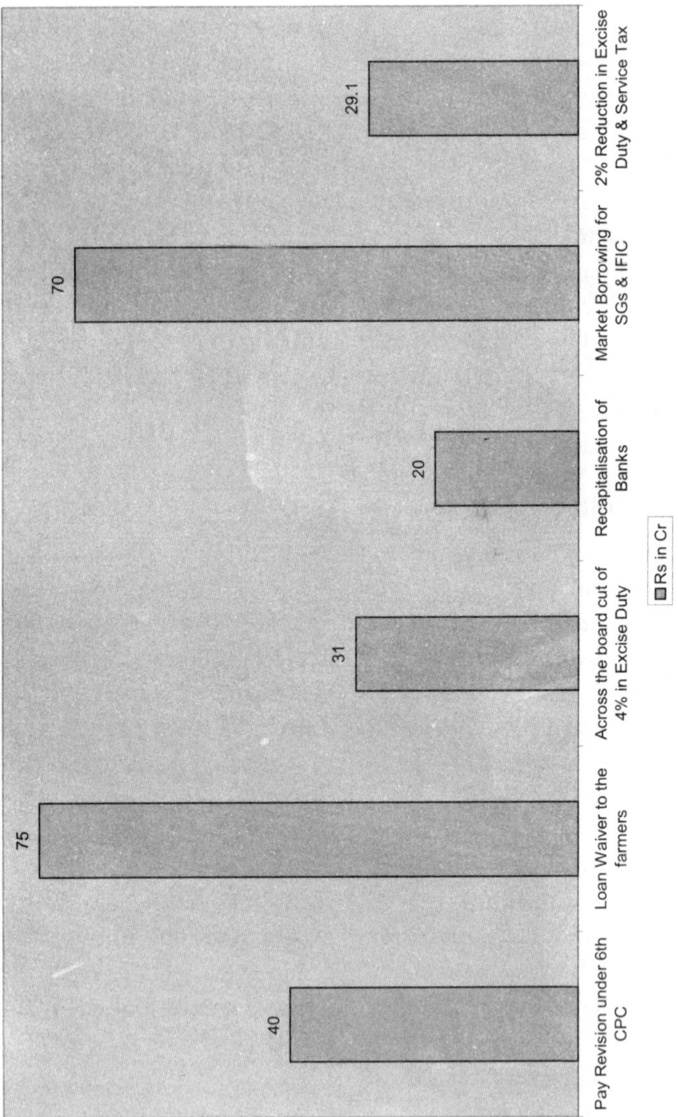

Fig. 5.2. Cost of the Fiscal Stimulus Packages.

due to a salary hike for the government staff to the tune of Rs. 41,000 crores with the implementation of Sixth Central Pay Commission (CPC), debt waiver scheme for farmers estimated Rs. 75,000 crores, additional provision of funds for food and fertilizer subsidies, additional allocation under the plan for Centrally-sponsored Schemes (CSS) like the National Rural Employment Guarantee Scheme (NREGA). These additional expenses though not forms a part of stimulus package still serves as stimulus to the economy. There were also off-budget items like the issue of oil bonds and fertilizer bonds which had to be added to give a true picture of fiscal deficit in 2008-09.

Table 5.2. Trends of Fiscal Parameters during 2006-07 to 2010-11

	2006-07 Actual	2007-08 Actual	2008-09 Accounts	2009-10 Revised	2010-11 Budget
Centre					
Growth of Revenue Receipts	25.6	24.7	-0.3	6.9	18.2
Growth of Tax Revenue	30.6	25.2	0.9	4.9	14.8
Growth of Non-Tax Revenue	8.3	23.0	-5.3	15.7	32.0
Fiscal Deficit as % to GDP	3.3	2.6	6.0	6.7	5.5
Revenue Deficit as % to GDP	1.9	1.3	4.5	5.3	4.0
Primary Deficit as % to GDP	-0.2	-0.9	2.6	3.2	1.9
All States					
Fiscal Deficit as % to GDP	1.8	1.5	2.6	3.2	
Revenue Deficit as % to GDP	-0.6	-0.9	-0.2	0.5	
Primary Deficit as % to GDP	-0.4	-0.5	0.7	1.3	

Source: Budget Document, GoI & State Finances: A Study of Budgets 2009-10, RBI, 2010

The focus of fiscal strategy in post-Lehman collapse has been administering a growth stimulus package. The fiscal stabilisation process and the strict adherence to the Fiscal Responsibility and Budget Management (FRBM) Act has been relegated to the background. The States too have been allowed a relaxation in their fiscal and revenue deficit targets.

The situation changed drastically in 2009-10: the fiscal deficit shot up to 6.7 per cent of GDP, the revenue deficit touched a high of 5.3 per cent of GDP and the primary surplus turned into a deficit of 3.2 per cent of GDP. At the state level the fiscal deficit has raised to 3.2 per cent of GSDP in 2009-10 from a low of 1.8 per cent in 2006-07. The revenue surplus of last three years turned to a deficit (0.5 per cent of GSDP). Primary surplus also vanished and becomes a deficit to the tune of 1.3 per cent of GSDP.

Conclusion

There are now visible signs of recovery indicated by the emergence of manufacturing from stagnant or negative growth, the strong rally in equity markets, the huge mobilisation of funds by private corporates from the capital market etc. However, the poor monsoon this year is casting a shadow on recovery. The impact of monetary loosening, which happens with a lag, has perhaps begun as is seen from the recovery of manufacturing growth. The fiscal stimulus has helped in substituting for lost private demand to some extent and prevented a steeper fall in GDP growth. However, there is virtually no more fiscal and monetary policy space left to further stimulate growth.

REFERENCES

Budget at a Glance, 2010-11, Ministry of Finance, Government of India.

Joseph. M *et al.*, 2009, *The State of the Indian Economy, 2009-10*, Working Paper No 241, Indian Council for Research on International Economic Relations.

Mohan, T.T. Ram, 2009, The Impact of the Crisis on the Indian Economy, *Economic & Political Weekly,* March 28.

National Accounts Statistics, various issues, Central Statistical Organisation (CSO), GoI.

Rakshit, M, 2009, India amidst the Global Crisis, *Economic and Political Weekly,* March 28.

State Finances: A Study of Budgets 2009-10, Reserve Bank of India, 2010.

CHAPTER

Impact of Global Financial Crisis on South Asia : A View

Dr. P. Muthaiyan
Dr. A. Abdul Raheem
K. Sambasivam

ABSTRACT

The global financial crisis worsened their macro-economic difficulties as sources of funding contracted. Although India was well advanced in responding to the food and fuel price crisis and has generally maintained prudent macroeconomic management, the magnitude of the financial crisis has hit India very hard because of the strong connectivity to global financial markets. Bangladesh, Nepal, and Bhutan have been mostly insulated from the first round effects of the financial crisis owing partly to sound macro-economic management, but also because of the underdeveloped nature of the financial markets that are not well connected to international markets. They are however vulnerable to the second round effects of a global economic slowdown working through export earnings, tourism receipts, remittances and external financing for infrastructure. Issues in Afghanistan are much more complex and relate more to security and the political environment rather than the impact of global financial crisis. The recent slide in food and fuel prices has provided South Asia with a welcome relief. But overall, the evidence suggests that growth, investment, exports and employment have been hurt. The outlook for 2009 is bleak as the global downturn deepens further. Growth in South Asia decelerated in 2008, falling from 8 per cent in 2007 to 6 percent. It is projected to decline to 5 per cent in 2009, before recovering to 6 per cent in 2010. Therefore, this paper views on impact of global financial crisis on south Asia.

INTRODUCTION

The global financial crisis hit South Asia at a time when it had barely recovered from severe terms of trade shock resulting from the global food and fuel price crisis. The food and fuel price shocks had badly affected South Asia, with cumulative income loss ranging from 34 per cent of 2002 GDP for Maldives to eight per cent for Bangladesh. Current account and fiscal balances worsened sharply and inflation surged to unprecedented levels. Pakistan, Sri Lanka, and Maldives were particularly vulnerable because difficult political and social environments prevented adequate policy measures to adjust to the terms of trade shock. Additionally, their reliance on foreign funding has been relatively large. The global financial crisis worsened their macro-economic difficulties as sources of funding contracted. Although India was well-advanced in responding to the food and fuel price crisis and has generally maintained prudent macroeconomic management, the magnitude of the financial crisis has hit India very hard because of the strong connectivity to global financial markets. Bangladesh, Nepal, and Bhutan have been mostly insulated from the first round effects of the financial crisis owing partly to sound macroeconomic management, but also because of the underdeveloped nature of the financial markets that are not well connected to international markets. They are however vulnerable to the second round effects of a global economic slowdown working through export earnings, tourism receipts, remittances and external financing for infrastructure. Issues in Afghanistan are much more complex and relate more to security and the political environment rather than the impact of global financial crisis. The recent slide in food and fuel prices has provided South

Asia with a welcome relief. But overall, the evidence suggests that growth, investment, exports and employment have been hurt. The outlook for 2009 is bleak as the global downturn deepens further. Growth in South Asia decelerated in 2008, falling from 8 per cent in 2007 to 6 per cent. It is projected to decline to 5 per cent in 2009, before recovering to 6 per cent in 2010. Therefore, this paper views on impact of global financial crisis on South Asia.

GLOBAL FINANCIAL CRISIS IN SOUTH ASIA

India

India, South Asia's largest economy, has been facing major challenges owing to the global financial crisis. The immediate effects were plummeting stock prices, a net outflow of foreign capital, a large reduction in foreign reserves and a sharp tightening of domestic liquidity. These caused a rapid depreciation of the exchange rate and a surge in short-term interest rates. The second round effects emerged from a slowdown in domestic demand and exports. Demand effects have been particularly severe in housing, construction, consumer durables and the IT sector. As a result, manufacturing production has taken a hit and activities in the organized services sector (housing, construction, IT) are down sharply. Exports declined for two consecutive months in October and November 2008. A government study estimates job losses to the tune of five hundred thousand between October and December 2008. The GDP growth rate is now estimated at around seven per cent for 2008, down from nine per cent in 2007, and is projected to decline to around five per cent in 2009. The government of India has been highly proactive in managing this ongoing crisis with a slew of monetary and fiscal measures to stabilize the financial sector, ensure adequate liquidity, and stimulate domestic demand. The monetary policy measures have succeeded in stabilizing interest rates and the availability of domestic liquidity. The exchange rate has also stabilized and capital outflows have been contained, with foreign exchange reserves maintained at around $250 billion level. The pressure on the financial sector has been eased, although there is some evidence of an increase in non-performing loans. However, the financial sector has become more risk-averse. The decline in global fuel and other commodity prices has helped the balance of payments and lowered inflation, which has fallen sharply from a peak of 13 per cent in July 2008 to below six per cent in December 2008. This has created the space for monetary easing as well as providing better scope for the fiscal stimulus. The monetary and fiscal stimulus package is expected to contain the downward slide in demand in 2009 while providing a good basis for recovery in 2010.

Pakistan

Pakistan's economy has been under strain due to excess demand pressures that have been building since 2004. The combined effects of global food, fuel and financial crisis took quite a toll on the economy as the current account balance and fiscal deficits increased, inflation surged and South Asia Region, The World Bank Group February 17, 2009 3/6 growth slowed. Fortunately, strong corrective actions have been taken over the past few months including an IMF programme in November that is helping stabilize the Pakistani economy. Macro-economic imbalances are showing signs of improvement while inflation is easing. But economic growth has taken a hit, with growth slowing down from 7.3 per cent during 2004-07 to 5.8 per cent in 2008 and projected to slide to around 3 percent in 2009. The scope for counter cyclical fiscal policy is limited at this time, but Pakistan is taking measures to protect social spending to help reduce the adverse effects of the crisis on the poor. The story in Sri Lanka and Maldives is worrisome. Like Pakistan, these countries have been struggling with excess demand pressures, which have been further aggravated by the global food, fuel and financial crises.

Sri Lanka

Sri Lanka has taken actions to reduce monetary growth and contain the fiscal deficit. This, along with lower commodity prices, has helped reduce inflation, which has come down sharply from a peak of 28 percent in June 2008 to 11 percent in January 2009. But Sri Lanka's balance of payments is under stress, as current account deficit surged to about 7.5 per cent of GDP in 2008 and reserves have now fallen to less than 2 months of imports. Access to foreign commercial credit has also been sharply curtailed by the rapid rise in the cost of borrowing. Economic growth has come down from seven per cent during 2006-2007 to 6 per cent in 2008 and expected to decline to four per cent in 2009. Further actions are needed to stabilize the external economy to provide the basis for recovery of growth in 2010.

Maldives

Maldives is still grappling with major fiscal and current account imbalances, which has been further hurt by a slowdown in foreign private capital inflows and deceleration in the tourism sector. The new government is looking at ways to bring the macro economy back on track. South Asia Region, The World Bank Group February 17, 2009 4/6 Evidence from other South Asian countries that are not well connected to global financial markets—Bangladesh, Bhutan, and Nepal—show that the direct first round effects of the global financial crisis have been muted.

Bangladesh

Bangladesh has held up remarkably well due to deft economic management that helped absorb the pressure of the global food and oil price crisis of the January 2007-May 2008 period without jeopardizing macroeconomic stability. Although stock prices have fallen, domestic liquidity seems adequate. Domestic interest rates, both long-term and short-term, are stable. Exports for the first 6 months of the fiscal year (July-December) have grown at a healthy pace of 19 per cent and remittance inflows show a 31 per cent increase. The recent decline in global commodity prices, especially food and fuel, is helping ease inflationary pressure while also providing a welcome increase in the fiscal space and balance of payments.

Bhutan

Bhutan's economy is closely tied to India. Since there are no indications of reductions in aid or delays in the development of the next mega-hydropower projects, the macroeconomic underpinnings appear sound. The banking system has adequate liquidity, reserves are at a high level (exceeding 14 months of imports), and the authorities continue to make good progress with implementing their reform program. Second round effects are expected, however, with growing non-performing loans and weaker tourism activity later in 2009.

Nepal

Nepal is benefitting from higher inflows of remittances and healthy availability of foreign aid. Along with the decline in global commodity prices, the balance of payments and fiscal situation are comfortable and there is no evidence of a liquidity constraint on domestic demand. On the contrary, the large foreign exchange inflows are creating some demand pressure that has contributed to a surge in inflation that requires better management. South Asia Region, the World Bank Group February 17, 2009 5/6.

REDUCE THE ADVERSE EFFECTS OF THE FINANCIAL CRISIS

Nevertheless, there is no room for complacency for any South Asian countries. While Bangladesh's overall exports for the first six months show strong growth, exports during October-December 2008 actually declined by 1.4 per cent over the same period in 2007 as compared with 42 per cent growth during July-September, indicating a worrisome outcome. Importantly, the adverse effects of the global economic slowdown are still emerging, especially given the growth outlook for industrial economies for 2009. In addition to lower demand, there is strong evidence of a trade credit crunch. So, the spillover negative effects for developing country exports including South Asia can be very large. There are also populist pressures in industrial countries for trade protection that could further hurt South Asia's export prospects in 2009 and beyond. Similarly, while remittances are holding up well so far, the sharp decline in oil prices will likely reduce the demand for additional migrant labor in the oil-rich Arab countries and could hurt remittance income in the coming months.

Moving forward, the South Asian countries can do a number of things to reduce the adverse effects of the financial crisis and prepare the way for a resumption of rapid growth in 2010. First, policy attention needs to focus on creating as much additional fiscal space as possible to prop up the domestic economy while preserving macro-economic stability. As noted, the decline in global fuel and food prices has provided a welcome opportunity to regain the loss in fiscal space owing to previous higher prices. This gain should not be wasted in reversing the policy changes made in aligning domestic prices better to the global prices, especially domestic fuel prices. Additionally, efforts must intensify to raise public revenues. All South Asian countries have scope for raising revenues through strengthening tax compliance and aligning better public utility prices to their production costs. Second, a careful look at expenditure priorities is in order. Public spending that creates jobs, especially for the poor, will be essential. Important examples include rural and other infrastructure (rural roads, irrigation facilities, rural power); basic urban services; and well-designed safety net programs. Third, the ongoing efforts to increase the efficiency and effectiveness of the banking sector must continue. These measures should aim to lower intermediation cost, reduce non-performing loans, improve banking services, and strengthen prudential regulations.

Fourth, in the face of sliding world demand, efforts to raise domestic productivity and competitiveness become critical factors for protecting export market shares. The scope for increasing the competitiveness of the South Asian economies is large and includes policies to improve the availability of infrastructure, lower the transaction cost of private investment through better governance, and reduce restrictions on trade and investment. Finally, in an environment of constrained resources, greater attention to improving implementation capacity and corruption prevention in public spending becomes even more important.

REFERENCES

Henry, Peter Blair (2007), "Capital Account Liberalization: Theory, Evidence, and Speculation", *Journal of Economic Literature*, Vol. XLV, December.

International Monetary Fund (2008a), *"Global Financial Stability Report"*, October.

IMF (2008b), "World Economic Outlook", October.

Mohan, Rakesh (2006), "Coping With Liquidity Management in India: A Practitioner's View", *Reserve Bank of India Bulletin,* April.

IMF (2007a), "Development of Financial Markets in India", *Reserve Bank of India Bulletin,* June.

IMF (2007b), "India's Financial Sector Reforms: Fostering Growth While Containing Risk", *Reserve Bank of India Bulletin,* December.

Prasad, Eswar S., Raghuram G. Rajan and Arvind Subramanian (2007), "Foreign Capital and Economic Growth", *Brookings Papers on Economic Activity,* 1.

Reserve Bank of India (2008), *Annual Policy Statement for the Year 2008-09, April, World Bank* (2008), "Global Development Finance 2008", June.

CHAPTER

Impact of Social Responsibility Informtion on Investors' Investment Decision : An Empirical Evidence from India

A.N. Shankar
N.M. Panda

ABSTRACT

Over a period of three decades academicians and policy-makers across the globe raise a number of important issues with which the social investment movement, social research firms, and academics have been struggling. Socially responsible investing (SRI) and social researchers who support it, as well as academic researchers who use the data generated by social research, recognise that the gathering and use of company data of any sort is an ongoing process of continual improvement and focusing in the field of social accounting research. In Indian context limited number of studies were conducted in this area, thus an attempt has been made to focus on the investors' preference for social responsibility information, that could pave way for future research and policy making by apex bodies to incorporate clauses essential for appropriate presentation of corporate social responsibility information along with financial information. This paper is designed to find whether there exists preference for social responsibility information in investment decision making, if yes, which type and theme of social responsibility information is perceived significant by investors.

The outcomes reveal the apparent significance of social responsibility disclosure for investors and preference of such information varies across themes and type of social responsibility information.

KEY WORDS

Corporate Social Responsibility, Social Responsibility Disclosure, Investors' Perception, CSR Themes.

INTRODUCTION

Corporate social responsibility (CSR) has attracted considerable attention during the past five decades. However, discussions on social responsibility have, for the most part, been very limited in scope (Alexander and Buchholz, 1978;[1] Carroll, 1979;[2] Edmunds, 1977;[3] Gatewood and Carroll, 1981[4]; Goodpaster and Matthews, 1982;[5] Keim, 1978;[6] Miller and Sturdivant, 1977;[7] Rudd, 1981;[8] Sethi, 1975;[9] Shocker and Sethi, 1973;[10] Tuzzolino and Armandi, 1981;[11] Zenisek, 1979[12]). Little consideration has been given to the development of a CSR framework that integrates both content and the process concepts. Although milestones toward a theory of corporate social performance (CSP) can be identified (Carroll, 1979;[13] Freeman, 1984;[14] Miles, 1987;[15] Wartick and Cochran, 1985[16]), there is not yet such a comprehensive theory on it is still awaited. Conceptual developments have not been systematically integrated with one another, but usually have been treated as free standing, implicitly competing ideas. Thus, a vast, diverse, and interesting field of research and theory has been generated, but there is no means for assessing the relevance of all these works to the field's central concerns. Therefore, management is hampered by the lack of a paradigm which addresses both the "what" and the "how" of corporate social behaviour. Furthermore, although management researchers recognise that CSR has strategic implications for the firm; few have focused on the interdependent and dynamic relationships among the firm and the relevant actors in its social environment. Investors' decision undeniably affects firms' financial position; they are the key actors in prioritising firms and play a role in channelising firms' internal and external activities. In order to attract funds with minimal efforts corporate bodies usually portray a rosy picture. Studies abroad have revealed that, investors to some extent do incorporate social responsibility disclosure (SRD) in their investment decision making. In Indian context such works are in dearth, more over in entirety it is observed that sleek literature is existing in the area of the type of SRD preferred by investors. This paper is designed to focus on the impact of SRD on prospective institutional investors' in investment decision making in Indian context with a little insight into the preferred type of SRD information. Once known the nature and type of SRD information preferred at policy making hierarchy it will be convenient to design a concrete standardised structure for CSR disclosure that could help corporate bodies and stakeholders to perform and disclose information.

Brief Review of Literature

Globalization has increased calls for corporations to use firms' resources to help alleviate a wide variety of social problems. Firms engaged in manufacturing are encouraged to apply developed nations laws and norms to issues such as child labour and environmental pollution in less developed countries, regardless of local laws or customs. Simon *et al.* (1972),[17] contend that there are "ethical investors" willing to pay a premium for the securities of socially conscious firms. This "ethical" behaviour may be economic as well as altruistic. Only firms that have gained the goodwill of the general public and are ideal corporate citizens, could develop these intangible assets into strategic advantages (Krishan and Balchandran (2005).[18] Such a need for expanded responsibilities of business is innately appealing to those who see existing governments as unable or unwilling to deal with such problems. Firms may indeed have resources that could be used to help with issues that are traditionally dealt with by governments or other non-governmental organisations. Participating in social issues not related to the firm's direct relationship with primary stakeholders, however, may not create value for shareholders (Hillman and Keim, 2001).[19]

Building better relations with primary stakeholders like employees, customers, suppliers, and communities (Freeman, 1984)[20] could lead to increased financial returns by helping firms develop intangible but valuable assets which can be sources of competitive advantage. For example, investing in stakeholder relations may lead to customer or supplier loyalty, reduced turnover among employees, or improved firm reputation (Hillman and Keim 2001). By developing long-term relationships with primary stakeholders, firms expand the set of values creating exchanges with stakeholder groups, beyond what is possible with interactions limited to market transactions. These valuable assets in turn lead to a positive relationship between stakeholder management and shareholder value wherein effective stakeholder management leads to improved financial performance.

Another theoretical question is the relationship between corporate social performance and investment risk. Spicer (1978),[21] for example, has argued that institutional investors consider low CSP firms to be riskier investments, and his findings support this thesis. This risk arises, *inter alia*, from the possibility of costly sanctions resulting from adverse legislative or regulatory actions, judicial decisions, or consumer retaliation. The possibility of such actions then leads investors to revise their perceptions of the probability distribution of future costs and revenues (Shane and

Spicer, 1983).[22] Spicer cites survey data that show "a seemingly widespread view within the investment community that a moderate to strong association does exist" (Spicer, 1978: 96) between the risk of a corporation and its attention to issues of social responsibility and noted that, in terms of the theory of finance, an investment in a company that is socially irresponsible could be inefficient. By choosing a similar but socially responsible company, an investor might achieve the same return with lesser risk. Investors are assumed to consider both risk and the return, and high social responsibility may reduce risk, thus providing an incentive for company managers to invest in positive CSP measures. According to efficient market theory (Fama, 1970), institutional investors consider both of the above arguments when determining the appropriate risk-adjusted discount rate to use in discounting future cash flows. Myopic institutional behaviour is related to the discount rate, and interpretation of CSP as a risk-reducing measure is related to risk adjustment. Efficient market theory suggests that investors consider the effect of publicly available information on both future cash flow and investment risk simultaneously. If a firm makes a major social performance investment in, say, pollution control that reduces cash flow but does not reduce risk, the present value of all future cash flows will be reduced and the stock may be sold in accordance with the predictions of myopic institutions theory. If, on the other hand, a firm makes the same investment but reduces the probability of adverse legal or regulatory action through CSP enhancement so that the risk-adjusted discount rate falls, then it is possible that the decline in the discount rate could more than compensate for the drop in cash flow, making the stock more attractive to investors. On balance, then, to predict the effect of a CSP-enhancing commitment by a firm, an investor needs to know the effects of the measure on both cash flow and risk. To the extent that the performance of firms is comparable, however, institutional investors will tend to choose less risky stocks from firms with strong social performance.

According to myopic institutions theory (Hansen and Hill, 1991),[23] institutional owners tend to be more mechanical and short-sighted than individual investors. This short-sightedness occurs, because institutional money managers must compete for accounts which are reviewed and rewarded on the basis of annual or even quarterly performance. Accordingly, it is assumed that their investment decisions will be based on the same short time horizons (Woolridge, 1988).[24] The theory is relevant to our study because investments in corporate social performance tend to be long-term (Mahapatra, 1984),[25] and so there may be an incompatibility between an institutional owner's time horizon and the time needed to realize the benefits from a commitment to CSP.

Teoh and Shiu (1990)[26] have examined the attitudes of institutional investors, particularly the fund managers toward corporate social performance and sources of information about it. They find that institutional investors do not normally alter their investment decisions on the basis of company assertions about CSP contained in conventional financial information, such as annual reports. However, institutional investors take CSP information into account if it is quantified, focused on specific issues, and obtained from disinterested parties.

Freedman and Stagliano (1991)[27] report that the stock price of firms in the cotton-textile industry is adversely affected by the Supreme Court's decision that validated a more stringent Occupational Safety and Health Administration (OSHA) standard for cotton dust emission. They decompose a sample of 27 companies into groups based on firms' prior disclosure of the potential impact of the standard on operations and find that the share price of firms that provided no disclosure or only narrative disclosure, or which simply reported that the standard would have only immaterial effects on operations, declined relative to companies that disclosed quantitative information about the standard's impact.

Blacconiere and Patten (1994)[28] have examined the stock market reaction to other chemical firms of the catastrophe of Union Carbide's chemical leak, which resulted in approximately 4,000 deaths and 200,000 injuries in Bhopal, India in December 1984. The study indicates evidence of a significant intra-industry reaction. However, firms with more extensive environmental disclosures in their financial report prior to the chemical leak have experienced a less negative reaction than firms with less extensive disclosures. The result suggests that investors interpreted such disclosures as a positive sign of the firm managing its exposure to future regulatory cost.

Shane (1995)[29] investigates shareholder wealth effects of changes in environmental regulation ushered in with the Clean Air Act Amendments of 1970. His sample of 47 firms that employed polluting production processes experience an estimated 12 per cent risk-adjusted decline in market value at the time leading to the change in environmental regulation. The statistically significant decline in shareholder wealth is consistent with market prices impounding information about expected compliance costs at a stage in the regulatory process earlier than that documented in prior literature.

Balabanis, *et al.,* (1998)[30] in their study find no empirical support for the hypothesis that "ethical investors consider corporate social information". Quite opposite, their findings suggest that the capital market seems to be rather indifferent to firms that undertake some CSR activities. Interestingly, their results show that a firm disclosing CSR information leads to negative impact on capital market participants. While there is an increase in the supply of environmental information in the companies' annual report, research has also found a demand for environmental performance information that is not being met by current reporting practices (Deegan and Rankin, 1996).[31] In other words, there exists a significant '*expectation gap*' between the users and preparers of financial statements.

Study by Zajac and Westphal(2004)[32] discloses that the institutional investors are influenced by the policy information of the companies and also by how does the information content internal or external confirms its practice in the implementation process, affects the stock market performance likewise the non-conformity of information does have adverse affect on market value of the company. Thus institutional investors' perception of ethical behaviour of corporation is essential in investment decision context.

Innovest Group(2007)[33] conducted a survey pertaining to Environmental disclosure in particular using the Carbon Beta as the index of a company associated with the financial performance measures, and investors interest in disclosures pertaining to environmental impacts of ongoing projects and prospective projects. One of the proposition statistically tested by the group was "There is strong evidence of dramatic increases in the level of institutional investor concern and intervention with climate change issues and their investee companies". The trend for investors' interest in environmental impact information have been tested by the formation of three different groups of concerned institutional investors: Namely '*The Carbon Disclosure Project*' a global coalition comprising of over 300 institutional investors, with combined assets of over $40 trillion, '*The Investor Network on Climate Risk (INCR)*', comprising of over 50 U.S. institutional investors[34] and '*The Institutional Investor Group on Climate Change*' includes over 35 of the leading institutional investors in Europe. In the mega survey comprising of 1500 companies spread over 800 sectors it is discovered that investors rely more on information about environmental disclosures made by third party

(Professional Agency) rather than company annual reports as annual reports may be subjective and are prone to window dressing.

The inconclusive arguments and empirical results obtained from the review of literature regarding the question whether social responsibility disclosure influence the investors' investment decision have prompted us to formulate the fourth objective of the study as, to find out the effect of perceived importance of social responsibility information on the investment decisions by the investors in India. Accordingly, an experiment has been designed in this study following the methodology discussed in next section. The purpose of the experiment is to examine the acceptability of the following null hypotheses:

H_{0a}: There is no significant difference in the impact between financial information and financial plus general SRD information on investment decisions by investors.

H_{0b}: There is no significant difference in the perceived importance of (*i*) financial and non-financial forms of SRD and (*ii*) quantitative and narrative forms of SRD by investors for investment decision-making.

H_{0c}: There is no significant difference in the perceived importance of different themes of SRD by investors for investment decision-making.

Methodology

Experimental method has been adopted for pursuing the study. Experiment was conducted in two stages, where by one hundred subjects (100 MBA students with Finance Specialization) have been conveniently drawn from two business schools (42 subjects from Assam Institute of Management and 58 from North Eastern regional Institute of Management Studies) as surrogate of investors. The rationale behind the choice of such a group of surrogate investors is that they represent a more homogeneous group for the purpose of this analysis and that they are expected to have adequate professional knowledge and skills to make rational investment decisions.

Two sets of information cues have been prepared by using actual data from two companies within the same manufacturing industry and presented for two hypothetical companies A and B. Any confounding effect of market segment differences (Ingram 1978)[35] has been thus removed. The first set contains only financial information which comprises three year Comparative Balance-sheet and two year Profit and Loss statement with some financial highlights. The second set contains the same financial information but in addition, also includes some social responsibility disclosure (SRD) in narrative, and quantitative form for company A in the same manner as would appear in the annual report. For company B the information is provided with a conventional set of Comparative Financial Statements and financial highlights only (Appendix I and Appendix II).

Subjects were first randomly assigned between an experimental and a control group. Since responses by the subjects in the control group are not to be used in further analysis 60 per cent of subjects have been randomly assigned to the experimental group and only 40 per cent of subjects have been assigned to the control group. Each subject in the experimental group has been asked to assume the role of investor with a sum of Rs 100,000 to invest in company A and company B in a proportion to be decided after reviewing the conventional financial information provided for company A and Company B .

In the second stage the subjects then have been requested to review the second set of information which contains both conventional financial statements and SRD for Company A and to make a decision on how the funds should be allocated between Company A and Company B. The experimental group thus has been subject to a repeated measure procedure in which any subject differences in decision outcomes between the two experimental conditions could only be attributed to the impact of the additional social responsibility information disclosed. Other effects have been tested utilizing a methodology employed by Hendriks (1976).[36] Accordingly, the control group has been presented with a set of information cues containing both financial information and SRD identical to the second information set for company A as given to subjects in experimental group. In the similar manner as a subject in the experimental condition , each subject in the control group has been asked to make an investment decision concerning Company A and Company B. Absence of order effects has been established if no significant differences exists in the response scores for the control group and the experimental group for the second experimental condition. The design of the experiment has been diagrammatically presented (Fig. 7.1).

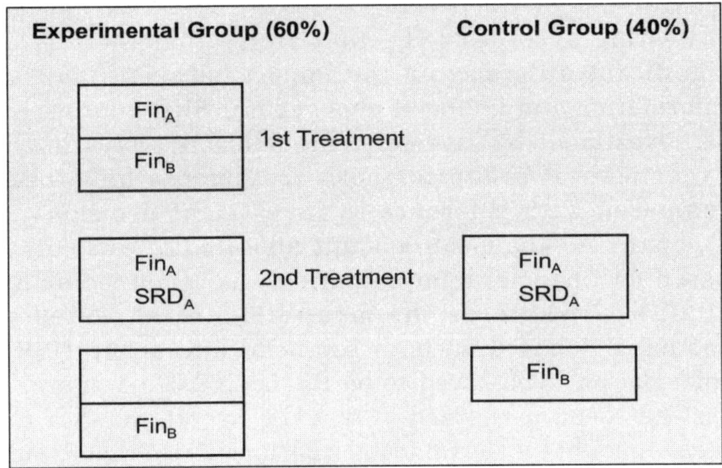

Note: Fin: Financial information
SRD: Social Information Disclosure
A and B stand for Company A and B respectively.

Fig. 7.1. Research design for the above objective

Analysis and Results

In the designed experiment 60 subjects from the experimental group received repeated treatments, at first with financial information only and then, financial information with SRD information. Forty subjects from the control group received only the second treatment, that is, financial information plus SRD information. The purpose of the control group is to control for order effects since all the subjects in the experimental group have received the financial information only as the first treatment. A test of the mean amounts allocated to company-A following financial information plus SRD information treatment by subjects in both the experimental and control groups, (Rs. 58,266.67 and Rs. 52,800 respectively) shows that there is no significant difference in the mean amounts ($t = 1.711$ for $d.f = 98$, $p < 0.09$). This suggests that the possibility of confounding due to order effects seems unlikely.

SRD Influence on Investment Decision (H_{0a})

In testing hypothesis H_{0a} that states that there is no significant difference in the impact between financial information and financial plus general SRD information on investment by investors, the subjects scores in the experimental group for both treatments have been compared with reference to investment decisions in Company A. The mean amount allocated to company A based on financial information only is computed at Rs. 49,081.67 where as the mean amount allocated to company A based on both financial and general SRD information is observed to be Rs. 58,266.67. A paired t-test has been performed to test the hypothesis that the mean amount for the financial information treatment only (*first treatment*) is not significantly different from the mean amount for the financial information plus SRD information treatment (*second treatment*). The result indicates that the null hypothesis (H_{0a}) of no significant difference stands rejected at 0.05 level of significance ($t = 4.823$, d.f = 59, $p < 0.000$). Further support for this conclusion is provided by performing a non-parametric Wilcoxon Matched-Pairs Sign –Rank test ($z = 4.513$ for $n = 60$, $p < 0.000$). Based on these results, it is inferred that the provision of general SRD information in addition to financial information has favourable (to company) impact on the investment decisions of investors.

Forms of Presentation of SRD (H_{0b})

Hypothesis H_{0b} states that there exists no significant difference in the perceived importance of (a) financial and non-financial forms of SRD and (b) quantitative and narrative forms of SRD by investors in their investment decision making. First the mean score for all the four forms of disclosure has been computed to represent as a measure of importance and then the respective standard deviation and coefficient of variation to indicate the representativeness of the mean scores (Table 7.1 and Fig. 7.2). The coefficients of variation being less than 30 in all the cases support the fact that all mean scores are the fair representatives of the sample.

Table 7.1. Importance of Different Forms of SRD on Investors' Decision

Form of Disclosure	Mean Score	Standard Deviation	Co-efficient of Variation
Financial	6.46	1.058	16.38
Non-Financial	5.01	1.078	21.52
Quantitative Non-Financial	5.45	1.158	21.25
Narrative Non-Financial	4.88	1.335	27.36

A cursory look at the table clearly reveals financial and quantitative disclosures are perceived to be more important than the non-financial and narrative form of disclosure. In order to ascertain the validity of the above hypothesis a paired t-test for means has been performed between the financial and non-financial forms of SRD for the whole sample (n = 100). The result indicates that there exists a significant difference in the perceived importance between the two forms of disclosure ($t = 8.801$ for $df = 99$, $p<0.000$) . Hence, on the basis of the result it is inferred that the financial SRD is perceived as more important for investment decisions than the non-financial SRD. Similarly another t-test has been performed to test the means of narrative and quantitative information forms of SRD for the whole sample. Again a significant difference is observed between these two types of SRD ($t = 4.08$ for $df = 99$, $p<0.0001$) which support the inference that quantitative disclosure shows a higher mean score than that for the narrative disclosure. The null hypothesis (H_{0b}) of no difference therefore stands rejected.

Themes of SRD (H_{0c})

Hypothesis H_{0c} states that there exists no significant difference in the perceived importance of different themes of SRD by the investors in their investment decisions. First

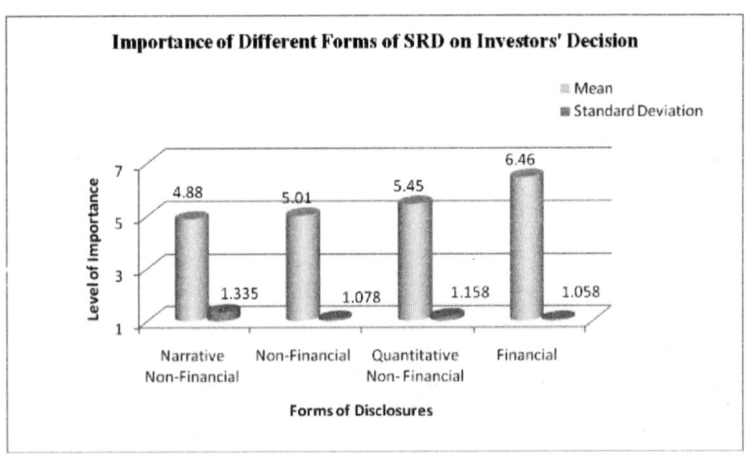

Fig. 7.2. Importance of Different Forms of SRD on Investor's Decesion

the mean score for all the themes of disclosure has been computed to represent as a measure of importance and then the respective standard deviation and coefficient of variation to indicate the representativeness of the mean scores (Table 7.2, and Fig. 7.3). The coefficients of variation being less than 30 in majority of the cases support the fact that all mean scores are the fair representatives of the sample. Subsequently one-way analysis of variance has been used to test this hypothesis. The results reveal that the mean scores computed for various themes of social responsibility disclosure are significantly different ($F = 27.260$, for $\upsilon_1 = 6$ and $\upsilon_2 = 693$, $p < 0.001$) thus leading to rejection of the null hypothesis H_{04c} of no difference in perceived importance of different themes of SRD by institutional investors. Profitability with mean = 6.45 is observed to be the most perceived important theme followed by growth with a mean score of 6.22 whereas rural development and urban affairs is perceived as the least important.

Table 7.2. Importance of Different SRD Themes on Investors' Decision

Form of Disclosure	Mean Score	Standard Deviation	Co-efficient of Variation
Profitability	6.45	0.833	12.91
Growth	6.22	0.927	14.90
People within	4.84	1.674	34.59
Rural Development	4.85	1.527	31.48
Environmental Affairs	5.28	1.386	26.25
Government	5.25	1.258	23.96
Economy	5.94	1.278	21.52

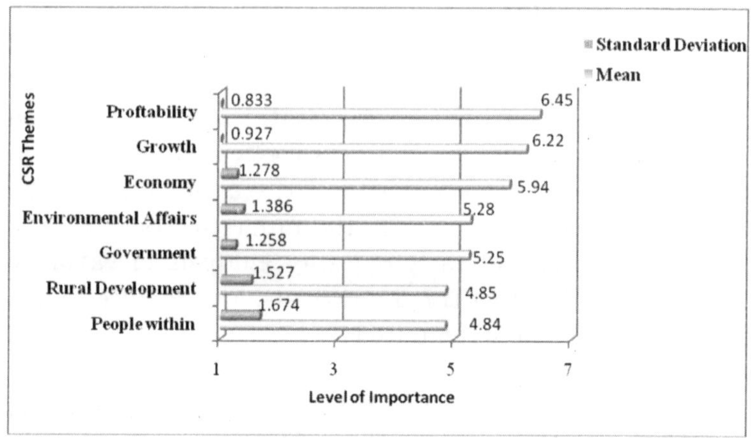

Fig. 7.3. Influence of Different SRD Themes on Investors' Decision

CONCLUSION

The experiment designed to find out the effect of perceived importance of social responsibility information on the investment decisions by the investors provides very interesting result. The result of the experiment does not support the null hypothesis (H_{0a}) that there is no significant difference in the impact between financial information and financial plus general SRD information on investment decisions by investors.

The study further reveals that financial and quantita-tive disclosures are perceived to be more important than the non-financial and narrative form of disclosure. The findings do not support the null hypothesis (H_{0b}) that there is no significant difference in the perceived importance of (*i*) financial and non-financial forms of SRD and (*ii*) quantitative and narrative forms of SRD by investors for investment decision-making. With regard to the influence of various themes, it is found that the perceived importance of a theme of social responsibility information varies from that of another theme. The hypothesis (H_{0c}) that there is no significant difference in the perceived importance of different themes of SRD by investors for investment decision-making stands rejected. Indian Investors still need further orientation towards more philanthropic and broad approach towards investing in firms as profitability is myopic objective where as attaining sustainability is ever ending approach.

It is observed in the experiment that the provision of general SRD information in addition to financial information has favourable (to company) impact on the investment decisions of the investors in India. The investors prefer financial forms of SRD to the non-financial and within non-financial form quantitative to narrative. Further, there is found a difference in the perceived importance of different themes of SRD by investors for investment decision-making.

Suggestions

This calls for not only the social performance but also for the communication of performance to those who are concerned and regarded as the stakeholders. Social responsibility may not be viewed as unidirectional activi-ties to always flow from the corporate firms; rather it should be viewed as a reciprocative phenomenon of exchange - where the members of the society-the shareholders, investors, employees, customers and even the general citizens need to reciprocate the socially responsible behaviour of the firms. This approach is based on reward and punishment and demands organic behaviour of the society as a whole in order to promote sustainable relationship among various constituents. There is adequate evidence in the study to focus on designing certain standardised quantitative measures to report the corporate social responsibility performance. Thus, it carries a mess-age for apex bodies to develop accounting standards for social responsibility performance reporting. Finally it's the obligation of educational institutions to incorporate a sense of corporate social responsibility amongst the learners for sustainable corporate future.

REFERENCES

Alexander, G J and Buchhloz, R A (1978), Corporate Social Responsibility and Stock Market Performance, *Academy of Management Journal*, 21(3), 479-486.

Carroll, A. B. (1979), A Three-Dimensional Conceptual Model of Corporate Performance. *Academy of Management Review*, 4(4), 497-505.

Edmunds, S. W. (1977), Unifying Concepts in Social Responsibility, *Academy of Management Review*, 2(1), 38-45.

Gatewood, E., and Carroll, A. B. (1981), The Anatomy of Corporate Social Response: The Rely, Firestone 500, and Pinto Cases. *Business Horizons*, 24(5), 9-16.

Goodpaster, K. E., and Matthews, J. B. (1982), Can a Corporation Have a Conscience? *Harvard Business Review*, 60(1), 132-141.

Keim, G. (1978), Corporate Social Responsibility: An Assessment of the Enlightened Self-interest Model. *Academy of Management Review*, 3(1), 32-39.

Miller, K. E., and Sturdivant, F. D. (1977), Consumer Responses to Socially Questionable Corporate Behaviour: An Empirical Test , *Journal of Consumer Research*, 4(1), 1-7.

Rudd, A. (1981), Social Responsibility and Portfolio Performance, *California Management Review*, 23(4), 55-61.

Sethi, C.F.S. (1975), Dimensions of Corporate Social Performance: An Analytical Framework, *California Management Review*, 17(1), 58-64.

Shocker, D and Sethi, P.S (1973), An Approach to Incorporating Social Performance in Developing Corporate Action Strategy , *California Management Review*,15(4), 97-105.

Tuzzolino Frank and Armandi, Barry R. (1981), A Need-Hierarchy Framework for Assessing Corporate Social Responsibility , *The Academy of Management Review*, 6(1), 21-28 Pub: Academy of Management.

Zenisek, T.J. (1979), Corporate Social Responsibility: A Conceptualization Based on Organisational Literature , *Academy of Management Review*, 4(3), 359-368.

Ibid.

Freeman, R. E.(1984), *Strategic Management: A Stakeholder Approach.*, Pitman Publishing. Boston, USA.

Miles, R. H. (1987), Managing the Corporate Social Environment: A Grounded Theory, Englewood Cliffs,: Prentice Hall., NJ, USA.

Wartick, S. L., and Cochran, P. L. (1985), The Evolution of the Corporate Social Performance Model, *Academy of Management Review*, 10(4), 758-769.

Simon, John G., Charles W. Powers, and Jon P. Gunnemann, (1972), *The Ethical Investor: Universities and Corporate Responsibility*, Yale University Press.

Krishan, S K and Balchandran, R. (2005), *Marketing Strategies for Firms in Emerging Markets* IIM K–NASMEI International Conference Kolkata.

Hillman, Amy J. and Keim, Gerald D . (2001), Shareholder Value, Stakeholder Management, and Social Issues: What is the Bottom Line? *Strategic Management Journal*, 22, 125-139.

Freeman (1984), *op cit.,* p. 19.

Spicer, B. H. (1978), Investors Corporate Social Performance and Information Disclosure: an Empirical Study, *Accounting Review*, 53(1), 94-111.

Shane, P. and Spicer, B. (1983), Market Response to Environmental Information Produced Outside the Firm , *The Accounting Review*, 58(2), 521-38.

Hansen, G. S. and Hill, C. W. L. (1991), Are Institutional Investors Myopic? A Time Series Study of Four Technology Driven Industries, *Strategic Management Journal*, 12, 1-16.

Woolridge, J. R. (1988). Competitive Decline and Corporate Restructuring: Is a Myopic Stock Market to Blame? *Journal of Applied Corporate Finance*, 1(Spring), 26-36.

Mahapatra, S. (1984), Investor Reaction to a Corporate Social Accounting, *Journal of Business Finance and Accounting*, 11, 29-40.

Teoh, H. Y., and Shiu, G. Y. (1990), Attitudes Towards Corporate Social Responsibility and Perceived Importance of Social Responsibility Information Characteristics in a Decision Context, *Journal of Business Ethics*, 9(1), 71-77.

Freedman, M., and Stagliano, A J (1991), Differences in Social-Cost Disclosures: A Market Test of Investor Reactions, *Accounting, Auditing and Accountability Journal,* 4(1), 68-83.

Blacconiere, W.G., and Patten, D.M. (1994), Environmental Disclosures, Regulatory Costs,and Changes in Firm Value, *Journal of Accounting and Economics,* 18, 357-377.

Shane, P.B.(1995), An Investigation of Shareholder Wealth Effects of Environmental Regulation, *Journal of Accounting, Auditing and Finance,* 10(3), 485-521.

Balabanis, G, Philips, H.C. and Lyall J, (1998) Corporate Social Responsibility and Economic Performance in The Top of British Companies: Are They Linked? *European Business Review,* 98(1), 25-44.

Deegan, C., and M. Rankin, (1996) Do Australian Companies Report Environmental News Objectively? An Analysis of Environmental Disclosures by Firms Prosecuted Successfully by the Environmental Protection Authority, *Accounting, Auditing and Accountability Journal,* 9(2), 50-67, 1996.

Zajac, Edward J. and Westphal, James D. (2004), The Social Construction of Market Value: Institutionalization and Learning Perspectives on Stock Market Reactions, *American Sociological Review*, 69(3),. 433-457.

innovestgroup.com(2007), http//www.i-ratings.innovestgroup.com/newsletters/Carbon Beta Webinar recording.html accessed on 05.08.08

INCR signatories include a number of U.S. State treasurers, as well as several leading labour funds with over $4 trillion in assets.

Ingram R W (1978), An Investigation of Information Content of (Certain) Social Responsibility Disclosures, *Journal of Accounting Research*, 16(2), 270-85.

Hendricks. G F. (1976), Achieving Corporate Social Responsibility, *The Academy of Management Review*, 1(1), 38-46.

Appendix-I

Company A : Comparative Balance Sheets As on 1st April

Amounts in Rs 000s

Particulars	2006	2007	2008
Issued Capital and Reserves	341,403	413,798	431,678
Non-Current Liabilities	100,536	83,658	103,349
Current Liabilities	269,718	317,379	216,312
Total Funds	**711,657**	**814,835**	**751,339**
Non-Current Assets	283,640	341,145	356,728
Current Assets	428,017	473,690	394,617
Total Assets	**711,657**	**814,835**	**751,339**

Company A : Comparative Income Statements For the Year Ended 31st March

Amounts in Rs 000s

Particulars	2006	2007	2008
Sales	1,171,790	1,301,790	1,165,117
Operating profit before Income Tax	34,390	39,270	47,296
Income tax Expense	13,433	4,806	7,143
Operating profit before Extraordinary items	20,957	34,464	40,153
Extraordinary items	(8,606)	1,267	(1,590)
Net Profit for the year	12,351	35,731	38,563
Add: Unappropriated Profit brought forward	19,210	23,727	40,184
Transfer (to) and from reserves	1,842	(7,538)	4,820
Amount available for appropriation	33,403	51,920	83,567
Less: Dividends	9,676	11,736	12,751
Unappropriated Profits	23,727	40,184	70,816

Company A : Financial Highlights

Particulars	2006	2007	2008
Return on Shareholders' Fund (%)	6.8	9.5	10
Earnings Per Share (Rs)	32.5	53.2	61.9
Dividend Per Share (Rs)	15	19	20
Dividend Covered (times)	2.2	2.8	3.1
Net Tangible Asset Backing Per Share (Rs)	4.8	5.5	5.8
Debt/Equity (times)	108.3	96.1	75.4
Gearing (Total Liabilities/ Total Assets) (%)	52	49.2	42.5

Company B : Comparative Balance Sheets as on 1st April

Amounts in Rs 000s

Particulars	2006	2007	2008
Issued Capital and Reserves	158,688	180,020	205,553
Non-Current Liabilities	71,274	110,770	100,637
Current Liabilities	110,155	119,213	121,325
Total Funds	**340,087**	**410,003**	**427,515**
Non-Current Assets	177,871	223,819	237,557
Current Assets	162,216	186,184	189,958
Total Assets	**340,087**	**410,003**	**427,515**

Company B : Comparative Income Statements for the Year Ended 31st March

Amounts in Rs 000s

Particulars	2006	2007	2008
Issued Capital and Reserves	158,688	180,020	205,553
Sales	526,505	659,477	720,801
Operating profit before Income Tax	43,555	54,995	59,816
Income tax Expense	20,677	23,958	27,327
Operating profit before Extraordinary items	22,878	31,037	32,489
Extraordinary items	2,288	3,150	6,330
Net Profit for the year	25,166	34,187	38,819
Add: Unappropriated Profit brought forward	41,748	48,296	61,115
Transfer (to) and from reserves	(5,963)	(7,411)	(6,090)
Amount available for appropriation	60,951	75,072	93,844
Less: Dividends	12,655	13,957	15,397
Unappropriated Profits	48,926	61,115	78,447

Company B : Financial Highlights

Particulars	2006	2007	2008
Return on Shareholders' Fund (%)	14.8	17.6	16
Earnings Per Share (Rs)	20.9	25.6	24.4
Dividend Per Share (Rs)	11	11	11
Dividend Covered (times)	1.8	2.2	2.1
Net Tangible Asset Backing Per Share (Rs)	142.5	147.9	156.7
Debt/ Equity (times)	42.2	60.9	47.4
Gearing (Total Liabilities/ Total Assets) (%)	53.5	56.1	51.9

Additional Information

1. *Profitability :* Our organisation has assumed a glorious stature as one of the most profitable in the country. This achievement stands on the rock-solid foundation of a strong physical performance and all round improvement in efficiency and operations.

Company A : Comparative Balance Sheets As on 1st April

Amounts in Rs 000s

Particulars	2006	2007	2008
Issued Capital and Reserves	341,403	413,798	431,678
Non-Current Liabilities	100,536	83,658	103,349
Current Liabilities	269,718	317,379	216,312
Total Funds	**711,657**	**814,835**	**751,339**
Non-Current Assets	283,640	341,145	356,728
Current Assets	428,017	473,690	394,617
Total Assets	**711,657**	**814,835**	**751,339**

Company A : Comparative Income Statements for the Year Ended 31st March

Amounts in Rs 000s

Particulars	2006	2007	2008
Sales	1,171,790	1,301,790	1,165,117
Operating profit before Income Tax	34,390	39,270	47,296
Income tax Expense	13,433	4,806	7,143
Operating profit before Extraordinary items	20,957	34,464	40,153
Extraordinary items	(8,606)	1,267	(1,590)
Net Profit for the year	12,351	35,731	38,563
Add: Unappropriated Profit brought forward	19,210	23,727	40,184
Transfer (to) and from reserves	1,842	(7,538)	4,820
Amount available for appropriation	33,403	51,920	83,567
Less: Dividends	9,676	11,736	12,751
Unappropriated Profits	23,727	40,184	70,816

Company A : Financial Highlights

Particulars	2006	2007	2008
Return on Shareholders' Fund (%)	6.8	9.5	10
Earnings Per Share (Rs)	32.5	53.2	61.9
Dividend Per Share (Rs)	15	19	20
Dividend Covered (times)	2.2	2.8	3.1
Net Tangible Asset Backing Per Share (Rs)	4.8	5.5	5.8
Debt/ Equity (times)	108.3	96.1	75.4
Gearing (Total Liabilities/ Total Assets) (%)	52	49.2	42.5

2. *Growth :* The year witnessed sustained global economic growth and strong demand for our product in the new emerging markets. Consolidation in industry was prompted by growth in emerging economies as well as increasing opportunities in new markets. The global consolidation in the industry has resulted in a mature and stable market behaviour and facilitated synergy in marketing efforts. Apparent product use is predicted to grow over 6%, world-wide, during 2007-08. Export earnings during the year at Rs.1454 Crores was higher by 85% over the previous year.

3. *People Within :* To offer our people a share in the value created by the organisation, we announced the Employee Stock Option Plan which we expect to roll out in FY08.The HR-Training Division in Pune was awarded the National Best Training Division award for the 8th time from the Government of India. The Company's Suggestion Scheme received the Excellence Award conferred by the Indian National Suggestion Schemes' Association (INSSAN).

4. *Rural Development and Urban Affairs:* The Company's Kargil Scholarship Scheme", floated specifically with

the purpose of assisting children of Kargil war heroes, has benefited children from 89 families of Army and the Air force personnel, in the first year of its inception. Company's Charitable Hospital, 82-bedded fully equipped hospital caters to an industrial and rural population in the Raigad district of Maharashtra. It provides for free outpatient and subsidised in-patient treatment for the needy. About 50 volunteers from each Unit are trained to address issues of road safety-create awareness, educate people and partner with the police to implement safety measures on the road.

5. *Environmental Affairs :* Company's manufacturing units have been pursuing a host of initiatives for water conservation; a check dam which can hold upto 30,000 KL of water was constructed, In another Unit, de-silting of existing ponds to enhance the storage capacity from 30,000 kl to 40,000 kl/season was done, The percolation of water from the pond into the ground ensures a stable water table in the area, positively impacting the growth of trees

6. *Government Action :* Presidential Directives on Schedule Castes and Scheduled Tribes continued to be implemented and monitored on regular basis. Out of the total manpower, 14.93 per cent were Scheduled Castes and 11.33 per cent were Scheduled Tribes. The Company continued to pay thrust on implementation of Official Language Policy of Government of India. Our company strengthened its initiatives in various areas of Income Generation at par with government to further the objective of economic value creation and economic self-reliance of the villages in the vicinity, primary tools used to encourage its target groups to earn a better livelihood were : Irrigation projects, Agri Extension projects, Animal Husbandry, Kruiler Farming, Floriculture, Vocational Training etc.

7. *Economy:* The foreign exchange reserves of the country increased to around US$ 150 billion at the end

of the fiscal year. Exports touched an all-time high of 1.17 million tonnes, although with strengthening of the domestic market we shifted our focus to meeting domestic demand, which gained further buoyancy towards the end of the year.

Company B : Comparative Balance Sheets as on 1st April

Amounts in Rs 000s

Particulars	2006	2007	2008
Issued Capital and Reserves	158,688	180,020	205,553
Non-Current Liabilities	71,274	110,770	100,637
Current Liabilities	110,155	119,213	121,325
Total Funds	**340,087**	**410,003**	**427,515**
Non-Current Assets	177,871	223,819	237,557
Current Assets	162,216	186,184	189,958
Total Assets	**340,087**	**410,003**	**427,515**

Company B : Comparative Income Statements For the Year Ended 31st March

Amounts in Rs 000s

Particulars	2006	2007	2008
1	2	3	4
Sales	526,505	659,477	720,801
Operating profit before Income Tax	43,555	54,995	59,816
Income tax Expense	20,677	23,958	27,327
Operating profit before Extraordinary items	22,878	31,037	32,489
Extraordinary items	2,288	3,150	6,330
Net Profit for the year	25,166	34,187	38,819

1	2	3	4
Add: Unappropriated Profit brought forward	41,748	48,296	61,115
Transfer (to) and from reserves	(5,963)	(7,411)	(6,090)
Amount available for appropriation	60,951	75,072	93,844
Less: Dividends	12,655	13,957	15,397
Unappropriated Profits	48,926	61,115	78,447

Company B : Financial Highlights

Particulars	2006	2007	2008
Return on Shareholders' Fund (%)	14.8	17.6	16
Earnings Per Share (Rs)	20.9	25.6	24.4
Dividend Per Share (Rs)	11	11	11
Dividend Covered (times)	1.8	2.2	2.1
Net Tangible Asset Backing Per Share (Rs)	142.5	147.9	156.7
Debt/ Equity (times)	42.2	60.9	47.4
Gearing (Total Liabilities/ Total Assets) (%)	53.5	56.1	51.9

CHAPTER

Corporate Governance : Issues and Oppertunities for Financial Risk Management

Minaketan Dash
Sasikanta Tripathy

ABSTRACT

India is on a rapid economic growth path with past few years, average rates is still in stable position in spite of crisis and the contribution of banking sector is also significant. Overall there have been improved corporate earnings. This contribution is also being affected due to the improper management of financial risk. In this article the author is to give a bird's eye view about the concept of corporate governance and its ethical issues and opportunities for the practical application to mitigate financial risks in banking sector from Indian context of view by taking some practices in banks. Also the author is to analyze about the impact of this financial risks on our economical environment which is becoming one threat for our economical sustainability. At last it is concluded by highlighting the role of corporate governance in the modern competitive corporate sector which is the main aspect of environmental as well as economical development. As the sustainable development is not possible without the economical development so it is our obligation to focus on this financial risk management simultaneously with other aspect to keep on the ongoing process of sustainable development.

KEY WORDS

Corporate governance, economical sustainability, economic growth, sustainable development.

INTRODUCTION

India is on a rapid economic growth path with past three years' average rates being nine per cent and future projections for next five years being targeted at average 10 per cent. Overall there have been improved corporate earnings. Banking industry has traditionally been one of the most regulated ones in India. However, with opening up of the economy in most sectors, 1991 onwards, this industry has been no exception and has experienced a gradual phased deregulation. Several reforms have been initiated in this sector ranging from interest rate liberalisation to restructuring of the public sector banks to increased competition and hence efficiency. Banks today are expected to exhibit more discipline. In tune with this, the banking sector in India has undergone structural changes during the past decade. While previously there were mostly public sector banks (PSBs) providing vanilla-type plain services, today the sector is thriving with private banks, foreign banks and PSBs fighting it out in the streets with innovative approaches and services. To complete the competitive scenario, almost all global investment banks, hedge funds and private equity firms have been reaching out to corporate customers for investment funding. So as we have already faced a crisis regarding this type of mismanagement in banking sector also its return, we should not give that scope of management in corporate .

OBJECTIVES OF THE STUDY

1. Review about the concept of corporate governance.
2. To know about Its nature and characteristics.
3. What are the issues and opportunities for present corporate.

4. Importance of Corporate governance in banking scenario and its reforms.
5. The implementation of Corporate governance in banking sector.

METHODOLOGY OF THE STUDY

This aricle is based on literature aspect of corporate governance (CG), its nature as well as its issues and opportunities for corporate partially and for banking sector broadly. Also the author has discussed about its effectiveness in mitigation of risk in banking sector by highlighting some banking reforms as the evolution of traditional corporate governance. This article is an descriptive study and it sources of data are secondary sources like journals, magazine, articles and newspapers and publication.

REVIEW OF CONCEPT

Corporate governance is about ethical conduct in business. Ethics is concerned with the code of values and principles that enables a person to choose between right and wrong, and therefore, select from alternative courses of action. Further, ethical dilemmas arise from conflicting interests of the parties involved. In this regard, managers make decisions based on a set of principles influenced by the values, context and culture of the organisation. Ethical leadership is good for business as the organisation is seen to conduct its business in line with the expectations of all stakeholders. What constitutes good corporate governance will evolve with the changing circumstances of a company and must be tailored to meet these circumstances (OECD). There is therefore no one single model of Corporate Governance.

"Corporate Governance is the system by which companies are directed and managed. It influences how the objectives of the company are set and achieved, how risk is monitored and assessed and how performance is optimized. Sound Corporate Governance is therefore critical to enhance and retain investors' trust." *(Cadbury Report, 1992).*

ISSUES FOR CG

These are the issues or challenges arising in the business at the time of practicing corporate governance:

- Failures in board of member in taking decision and to understand the risk there firm is going to take.
- Conflicts between executive director and non executive director and senior executives at the time of decision making.
- Internal and external audit failure due to negligence or less support of executive member.
- Lack of transparency of business activity due to improper transaction and organizational structure which leads to less discloserment.
- The last not the least is the corporate culture which fosters unethical behavior and encourage unethical activity.

DIFFERENT ASPECTS OF CG

- Transparency (CSR).
- Stakeholder participation (Economical growth)
- Organizational participation (sustainable development)
- Accountability. (Environmental and social responsibility).

OPPORTUNITIES OF GOOD CG

Substantial development of robust regulatory structure and the rules of law. A strong sustainable economy with an ability to make a long term change. A willingness to embrace change at governmental as well as business level. Enhance good financial system and sustained financial market. Long-term benefits to the business and the economy and its comparative advantage. At the end we can say it will help the business to run in such a manner that the sustainable economic development can possible which is the main indicator of sustainable development.

IMPORTANCE OF CG IN BANKING SECTOR

The corporate governance of banks in developing economies is important for several reasons. First, banks have an overwhelmingly dominant position in developing-economy financial systems, and are extremely important engines of economic growth. Second, as financial markets are usually underdeveloped, banks in developing economies are typically the most important source of finance for the majority of firms. Third, as well as providing a generally accepted means of payment, banks in developing countries are usually the main depository for the economy's savings. Fourth, many developing economies have recently liberalised their banking systems through privatization/disinvestments and reducing the role of economic regulation. Consequently, managers of banks in these economies have obtained greater freedom in how they run their banks. In particular, the nature of the banking firm is such that regulation is necessary to protect depositors as well as the overall financial system. Using this insight, we examine the corporate governance of banks in developing economies in the context of ongoing banking reforms. We discuss the changing role of government in developing-economy banking systems and the consequences for corporate governances. The special nature of banking means that it is more appropriate to adopt the broader view of corporate governance for banks as well as the government intervention in order to restrain the behaviour of bank management.

SCOPE OF CG IN BANKS

- Discloser requirement.
- Listing rules requirement.
- Monitoring and enforcement.
- Proper regulatory interference such as Reserve Bank of India, SEBI and government rules and regulations.
- Transparency in business activity to its stakeholders and proper audit system to analyze the financial statement as per the S & P norms.

- Because operational activity is the main responsibility of banking business.

ISSUES IN PRACTISING CG IN BANKS IN MANAGING RISK

In many developing countries, the issue of bank corporate governance is complicated by extensive political intervention in the operation of the banking system. The pertinent issues that we briefly want to examine are government ownership of banks, distributional cartels, and restrictions on foreign bank entry. Government ownership of banks is a common feature in many developing economies. The reasons for such ownership may include solving the severe informational problems inherent in developing financial systems, aiding the development process or supporting vested interests and distributional cartels. With a government-owned bank, the severity of the conflict between depositors and managers very much depends upon the credibility of the government. However, given a credible government and political stability, there will be little conflict as the government ultimately guarantees deposits.

Risk management is the key issue in practising corporate governance in banking sector. The identifiable risk that is operational risk which can be properly managed by proper practice of corporate governance policy, that we can conclude by focusing on the scope of corporate governance like discloserment, transparency, governmental rules and different regulatory authority such Reserve Bank of India. We can detect the operational risk like :

- Cash management risk.
- Liquidity risk.
- Interest risk.
- Portfolio risk.
- NPA management risk.
- Credit risk.

All these types of risk can be mitigated by proper risk management tools, but to implement this tool corporate governance is most necessary as the board member as well as the management staff like the executives and non-executive staff will practice it in practical way. Also the cash management risk is totally depending on the bank regarding its financial status which can be studied by proper examination of financial statements.

The global financial crisis has revealed widespread and massive failures in risk management practices. Many economists, organisations and governments have suggested a link between poor risk management and corporate failings. The OECD acknowledged that although rating agencies, disclosure and accounting standards played a role in causing the credit crisis, the best boards used their own powers to overcome weaknesses and associated risks in these areas. Effective boards implemented systems which led to the efficient sharing of information and open dialogue across management and the board.

REFORMS IN CG

Reserve Bank of India has taken various steps furthering corporate governance in the Indian Banking System. These can broadly be classified into the following three categories: (*a*) Transparency; (*b*) Off-site surveillance; and (*c*) Prompt corrective action.

Transparency and disclosure standards are also important constituents of a sound corporate governance mechanism. Transparency and accounting standards in India have been enhanced to align with international best practices. However, there are many gaps in the disclosures in India *vis-à-vis* the international standards, particularly in the area of risk management strategies and risk parameters, risk concentrations, performance measures, component of capital structure, etc. Hence, the disclosure standards need to be further broad-based in consonance with improvements in the capability of market players to analyse the information objectively.

The *off-site surveillance mechanism* is also active in monitoring the movement of assets, its impact on capital adequacy and overall efficiency and adequacy of managerial practices in banks. The RBI also brings out the periodic data on "Peer Group Comparison" on critical ratios to maintain peer pressure for better performance and governance.

Prompt corrective action has been adopted by RBI as a part of core principles for effective banking supervision. As against a single trigger point based on capita adequacy normally adopted by many countries, Reserve Bank of India in keeping with Indian conditions have set two more trigger points namely Non-Performing Assets (NPA) and Return on Assets (ROA) as proxies for asset quality and profitability. These trigger points will enable the intervention of regulator through a set of mandatory action to stem further deterioration in the health of banks showing signs of weakness.

CG AS A SOCIAL RESPONSIBILITY

The CSR discourse advances a concept of business responsibility at odds with traditional notions of corporate governance. Corporate legitimacy is judged on the basis of the capacities of a company to increase equity value—a capacity that is secured by the appropriate distribution of rights and responsibilities between shareholder, board, and director– the concept of CSR sets out a broader notion of goals and of the means to attain them. Both views, narrow and broad, are recognised by the companies themselves. Thus, in their statement of *General Business Principles*, declares that

> "*We commit to contribute to sustainable development.* This requires balancing short and long-term interests and integrating economic, environmental and social considerations into business decision-making".

Findings

1. *Lay solid foundations for management and oversight* - Recognize and publish the respective roles and responsibilities of board and management.

2. *Structure the board to add value* - Have a board of an effective composition, size and commitment to adequately discharge its responsibilities and duties.
3. *Promote ethical and responsible decision-making* - Actively promote ethical and responsible decision-making.
4. *Safeguard integrity in financial reporting* - Have a structure to independently verify and safeguard the integrity of the company's financial reporting.
5. *Make timely and balanced disclosure* - Promote timely and balanced disclosure of all material matters Concerning the company.
6. *Respect the rights of shareholders* - Respect the rights of shareholders and facilitate the effective exercise of those rights.
7. *Recognize and manage risk* - Establish a sound system of risk oversight and management and internal control.
8. *Encourage enhanced performance* - Fairly review and actively encourage enhanced board and management effectiveness.
9. *Remunerate fairly and responsibly* - Ensure that the level and composition of remuneration is sufficient and reasonable and that its relationship to corporate and individual performance is defined.
10. *Recognize the legitimate interests of stakeholders* - Recognize legal and other obligations to all legitimate stakeholders.
11. *Corporate Governance Rating be* made mandatory for listed companies.

Conclusion

This article has argued that the special nature of banking institutions necessitates a broad view of corporate governance where regulation of banking activities is required to protect depositors. In developed economies, protection of depositors in a deregulated environment is typically provided by a system of prudential regulation, but in developing economies such protection is undermined by the lack of well-trained supervisors, inadequate disclosure requirements, the cost of raising bank capital. So corporate governance is not playing a risk management tool but also it is encouraging the economical activity for economical growth which most needed for sustainable development keeping social and environmental responsibility in eyes as these are the long term requirement for sustainability.

REFERENCES

Arun T.G.,&. Turner J. D, "Corporate Governance of Banks in Developing Economies: Concepts and Issues", pp. 5-10.

Adams, R. and H. Mehran, 2003, Is Corporate Governance different for Bank Holding Companies? FRBNY *Economic Policy Review*, April, 12-142.

Heremans Dirk, *"Corporate Governance Issues for Banks. A Financial Stability Perspective"*, pp. 3-11.

La Porta, R., Lopez-de-Silanes, F. and Shleifer, A. (1999), "Corporate Ownership Around the World", Journal of Finance, Vol. 54, pp. 471-517.

"Prabandhan" The Research Journal of ISBM, July 2009, pp. 3-17.

Velasquez G. Manuel. Fifth Edition, 2006. *"Business Ethics, Concepts and Cases"*, Pearson Publication, pp. 86-157.

"Vidwat" The Indian Journal of management, Volume 2, July-Dec 2009, p. 1-5.

CHAPTER

Sub-prime FIASCO : Its' Impact on Job Market

Sasikanta Tripathy

ABSTRACT

Sub-prime as the words define, means subordinate to primary. The words are used in the lending industry to define a borrower who does not have a good credit history and hence are not able to qualify for best market rates *vis-à-vis* the prime category borrower. The sub-prime crisis in US is the result of excessive amounts of loans made to people who could not afford them and excessive amounts of money thrown into the mortgage arena by investors who were very eager for high return. The crisis represents the other side of a phase when a low rate of interest, rising home prices and mortgage securitization brought huge gains. A number of factors such as legislations e.g. Community Reinvestment Act, low rate of interest, mortgage brokers and lenders, rating agencies played their role in generating crisis. Three important dimensions of the sub prime saga relate to poor regulation of investment banks, relaxation in lending standards led by greed in a regime of unbridled competition and failure of the asset market to realise the dues from the defaulter. It once again brings home the fact that financial sector is distinctive in nature and can be exposed to unbridled and unregulated competition only at the cost of a complete peril. In this paper the authors showcased an overview of Sub Prime Fiasco; it's pre-history, positive and negative impact on employment, opportunity for the job seekers.

KEY WORDS

Job Market, Sub-prime Fiasco, Mortgage

INTRODUCTION

Globalisation has ensured that the Indian economy and financial market can not stay insulated from the present financial crisis in the developed economy. In the light of the fact that the Indian economy is linked to global market through a full float in current account (trade and services) and partial float in capital account (debt and equity). The crisis in finance markets has rapidly become a global job crisis, which leads to unemployment. Global financial crisis affects our banking and financial market. It affects both capital as well as stock market. Basically it has a great impact on service sector particularly on IT sector. Companies on IT and financial sector continue the down size and cut costs and will not likely hire more people. It also affects the urban as well as the rural employment. This crisis not only has the the negative impact on employment in IT, banking and other sectors but also it provided ample of opportunities in BPO and health sectors. This global financial crisis has occurred due to the sub prime crisis.

Sub-prime as the words define, means subordinate to primary. The words is used in the lending industry to define a borrower who does not have a good credit history and hence are not able to qualify for best market rates *vis-à-vis* the prime category borrower. The term "sub-prime" reflects not the lending rate but the borrower's credit status. Potential sub-prime borrowers may comprise of financially troubled people, meaning thereby that the sub-prime lenders take a higher degree of risk. Hence, to offset the risk to an extent the lenders increase the interest rates.

BEGINNING OF SUB-PRIME CRISIS

The sub-prime lending refers to the lending to house borrowers with weak credit. Investment bankers and lenders in happy spree gave loan to the home loan buyers at minimal or zero down payment without proper credit verification. In the process demand rose stressing the crisis as a result the house prices began to rise. The interest cost in general started rising making the borrowing costly.

SUB-PRIME CRISIS

Sub-prime crisis means the problem faced by the money-lending institutions in getting back of loans from investors against their sub prime standard mortgages. This is mostly related to real estate sectors as more focused was being given on housing sector in America. Mainly since 1980s, during the rule of Bill Clinton and George W Bush, the faulty policies in American government had to weaker its economy like slow poison. So, that slow poison gradually aggravated the global economy today as sub prime crisis.

The financial crisis of 2007-2009 began in July 2007 when a loss of confidence by investors in the value of securitized mortgage in the United States resulted in a liquidity crisis that prompted a substantial injection of capital into financial markets by the United States Federal Reserve, Bank of England and the European Central Bank. The TED spread, an indicator of perceived credit risk in the general economy, spiked up in July 2007, remained volatile for a year, then spiked even higher in September 2008, reaching a record 4.65 per cent on October 10, 2008. In September 2008, the crisis deepened, as stock markets worldwide crashed and entered a period of high volatility, and a considerable number of banks, mortgage lenders and insurance companies failed.

The major reasons are :

(*a*) Imbalance occurrence of demand for and supply of money, goods and services.

(*b*) Operation of irregular movements of business cycles in global economy

(*c*) Sub-prime crisis by U.S.A. economy.

OBJECTIVES OF THE STUDY

The objectives of the present study is to find out:

1. A brief history of sub prime crisis,
2. The impact of this crisis on the job market,
3. Oppertunities for the job seekers,
4. Positive and negative impacts of global financial crisis on employment.

METHODOLOGY

This chapter enlightens the pre-history, objectives of the crisis started at U.S. which affected our country (India).

IMPACTS ON GLOBAL ECONOMY

The current economic crisis mostly generated by American economy affects the realty sector, banking sector, financial services, insurance, IT, and manufacturing sector in all-over the world :

- Some companies have started closed down their business due to weak financial position.
- Some companies are started to merge their business units with other financially sound companies in order to sustain their growth and stability in the market.
- Some also have started to cut-off the number of employees from its total workforce in order to achieve stable profit level in their business

The various affected companies are:

1. *Banking sector:* Lehman Brothers, Merill Lynch, Goldman Sachs, Citi Bank, ICICI Bank, HDFC Bank etc.

2. *Financial services sector:* India Bull, American Express, GE Money, Citi Finance etc.
3. *Insurance sector:* AIG, Forties, Metlife etc.
4. *Real Estate:* DLF, UNITECH, HCC etc.
5. *Manufacturing:* L & T, Ashok Leyland etc.
6. *IT sector:* Wipro, IBM, TCS, HCL Tech, Satyam Computer etc.
7. *Aviation:* Jet Airways, King Fisher Airlines etc.
8. *Automobiles:* GM, Ford, Chrysler etc.

Due to global recession the job market was affected severely, and its great impact becomes a challenge for all the job seekers as well as the fresher.

REASONS FOR JOB LOSS OR EMPLOYMENT OPPORTUNITY

- There is lack of practical exposures for skilled man power engaged in an organization.
- Due to global recession, there is out flow of foreign capital of about U.S. $10 billion from Indian market by FII. So, to divert some portion of profit for making payment to the FIIs, most companies related to foreign financial institutions are reducing their employees in India and America.
- The merger policies of various companies results in huge job loss in weaker companies.
- Faulty business practices employee behaviour in an organisation also affect the cases of losing jobs from that organization
- Again, due to global recession, the slow revenue growth and capital expenditure in various companies lead to the situation of laying off employees from their companies.
- The shortage of foreign exchange reserves also affects the international trade.

THE JOB MARKET HAS TAKEN THE BIGGEST DOWNTURN IN THE PAST EIGHT QUARTERS

The speed breakers are becoming more numerous on job street according to the Employment Outlook Survey (October-December 2008) the caution visible in the last quarter has turned into a decisive downturn - both in hiring and business sentiment. The employment outlook is down 10 index points while the business has dipped nine index points in the quarters (Fig. 9.1).

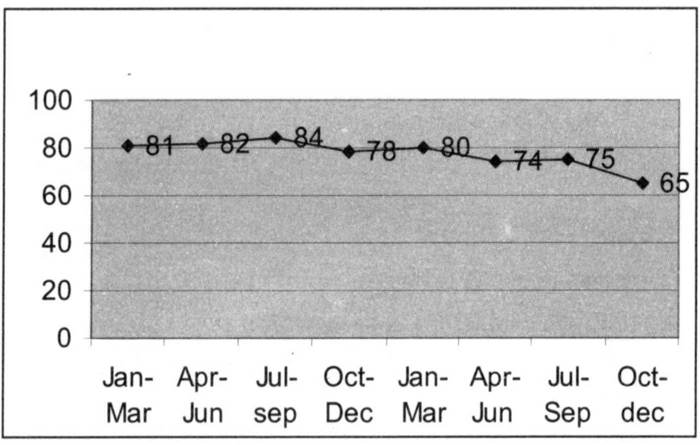

ITES STILL UPBEAT

Employers are in the wait 'n' watch mode. The result-hiring activity is likely to be sluggish in most sectors- IT, infrastructure, retail, FMCG and media, financial services, telecom and manufacturing and engineering. ITES is the only sector that is buoyant, according to the survey. However, this buoyancy has turned into caution after the Wall Street crash because many companies depend on the now sick U.S. financial services companies for major portions of their revenues. The survey, incidentally, was conducted before the crash. Companies are not talking layoff or even a freeze on hiring. Their focus has shifted towards improving efficiency and productivity of employees in order to remain competitive in the market, rather than on increasing staff strength (Fig. 9.2).

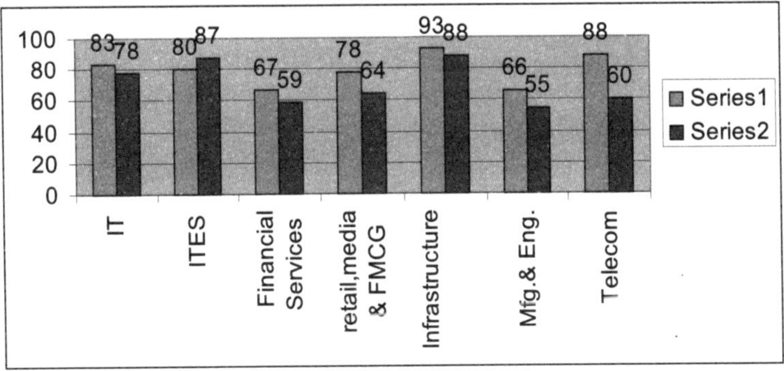

Fig. 9.2. TIES still upbeat : Sectorwise (Series 1 : 1 July – Sept. 2008 and Series 2 : 1 Oct. – Dec. 2008)

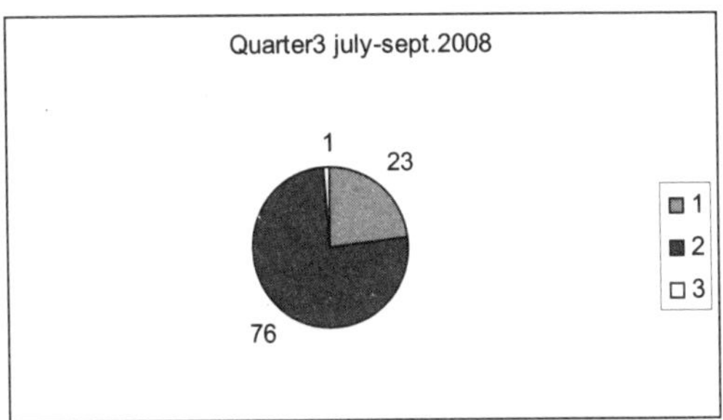

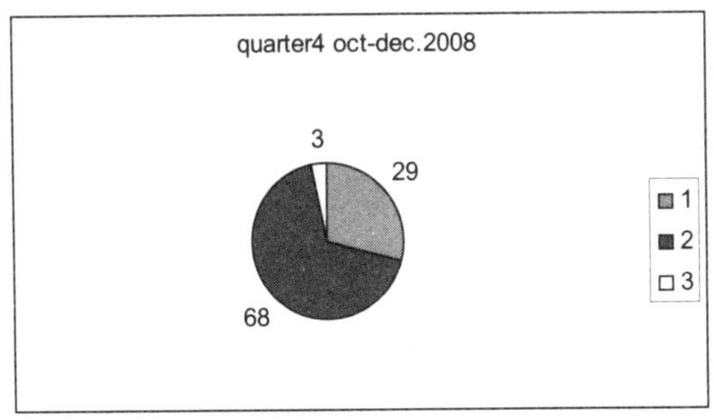

1-decrease, 2-increase, 3-no change
Fig. 9.3. Shrinking Job Pie

IMPACT OF JOB LOSS DUE TO FINANCIAL CRISIS

The impact of global financial meltdown on job cuts have been "limited" in India and that even the moderate economic growth is high enough to generate new employment opportunities.

The GDP growth rate is expected to moderate somewhat from a very high growth rate in the last three years, yet it remains sufficiently high this year generating new employment opportunities. The developed countries job losses due to global financial crisis has been limited in India as a large proportion of population is employed in the agriculture sector which has not been affected by the crisis. The services sector which makes up for a large share of the GDP has also been less affected. Even in the export sector, which registered negative growth in October, the fall was mainly due to a spike in export growth in October 2007 and is limited to some segments. While no exhaustive surveys have been conducted to estimate the likely job losses in India due to global economic crisis, a sample study of 121 export-related companies (for the period August-October 2008) by Department of Commerce has indicated fall in jobs due to slowdown in some export sectors. Indian economy including employment, he said it has taken several measures, financial and fiscal, to boost growth.

IMPACT ON EMPLOYMENT

Global slowdown in economic growth is expected to lead to significantly higher levels of unemployment. In major developed countries and export-oriented developing countries, unemployment is already on the rise as activities in finance, construction, automotive, manufacturing for export, tourism; services and real estate slow notably. The International Labor Organisation (ILO) estimated that the number of unemployed could rise by 20 million, reaching 210 million women and men by the end of 2009. The ranks of the working poor living on less than one dollar a day could swell by 40 million, while those on less than two dollars a day could increase by over 100 million. Although comprehensive data are still not available, the following are some indications of the severity of the unemployment situation in many countries.

In the United States, the latest government statistics indicate a total job loss of 2.6 million during 2008, bringing the unemployment rate to 7.2 per cent in December 2008, and the highest since January 1993. The number of persons unemployed for 27 weeks or more increased by 1.3 million in 2008. During the same period, the number of part-time workers who would like to work full-time also grew by 3.4 million. In China, an estimated 7,000 factories closed in the southern special economic zone of Shenzhen and Guangdong Province alone during 2008. Millions of laid-off migrant workers have returned home to the countryside. This is likely to result in reduced future remittances that have contributed to reducing poverty in rural areas while also adding pressure on rural unemployment and underemployment. The implication of job losses occurring in the immediate short term must be viewed in a long-term context. The current crisis is following a period of robust global economic growth, which some had described as "jobless growth", where job creation has not been sufficient to meet the demand for work by a growing global lab our force. Contractions in economic activities can be expected to worsen labour market conditions for workers, who have been facing increasing economic insecurity even during the economic boom. Slowing or even negative economic growth, together with volatile prices, will put great downward pressure on workers' real wages. ILO is predicting that wages in 2009 will likely decline by half of a percentage point in industrial countries while growing by about one per cent globally. While the economic downturn has taken a considerable toll on employment around the world, some social groups have been particularly affected. Today's youth bare the brunt of the unemployment problem. Even in times of relative economic prosperity, young people are already three times more likely to be unemployed than adults. In times of economic crisis, the youth employment predicament multiplies. Young people tend to be the last in and the first out, having not had the time to build long-standing relationships with their employers. Owing to their relative lack of work experience, contacts and job-search expertise, many youth will have difficulty finding new employment once they have been laid off.

At the other end of the age spectrum, older persons also face similar challenges in remaining in, or re-entering the labor market. Owing to their age, they face additional difficulties as many of them in developed countries have seen the value of their assets, including their retirement funds, pensions, savings and houses, decline drastically. At a time when food prices and health-care costs have increased, older persons will have to stretch their dwindling resources even further. For older persons in developing countries, most of whom are not covered under social security or other income schemes and many of whom remain in the labor market, their ability to sustain their livelihood, to compete for jobs and gain access to micro credit to sustain their own businesses will be further constrained. Furthermore, many of these older persons depend on younger family members for financial support. The loss of employment in urban areas and the expected decline in remittances will affect the well-being of the older household members left in rural areas.

Employment is an important channel through which the financial crisis is likely to affect indigenous peoples, who represent historically one of the poorest and most excluded social sectors in society. Similarly, migrant workers will face particular difficulties during a global economic downturn. In addition to higher unemployment and exclusion from social protection in host countries, they are likely to face heightened discrimination and rising xenophobia in difficult economic heightened discrimination and rising xenophobia in difficult economic times.

Evidence from past crises shows that economic recessions put a disproportionate burden on women, as women tend to have lower unemployment and social security benefits. In times of crises, women also take on additional responsibilities to provide non-market substitutes for market goods that their families are no longer able to afford. The review of the implementation of the Beijing Platform for Action in 2000 indicated that the economic and financial crises in Latin America, South Asia and Eastern Europe had hit the most vulnerable social groups hardest, and that women in particular had ended up with larger burdens of unpaid work. Women were especially affected by the resulting loss of jobs in the public sector and incurred increased responsibility for household care giving. During the Asian financial crisis in 1998, women were found to be disproportionately affected in the labor market. While both men and women were laid off, women were fired first as men were traditionally considered to be "breadwinners".

EFFECT OF FINANCIAL CRISIS ON VARIOUS COMPANIES & ITS EMPLOYMENT OPPORTUNITIES.

Employees Data of INFOSYS

Particulars	2008-09	2007-08	2006-07	2005-06	2004-05
Total Head count	73,490	59,831	44,658	32,178	23,377
Software Professionals	68,329	56,441	41,943	30,147	21,765
Support	5,161	3,390	2,715	2,031	1,612

Effects on Microsoft

Microsoft Corp. cuts 5000 jobs over the next 18 months, a sign of how badly even the biggest and richest companies are being stung by the recession.

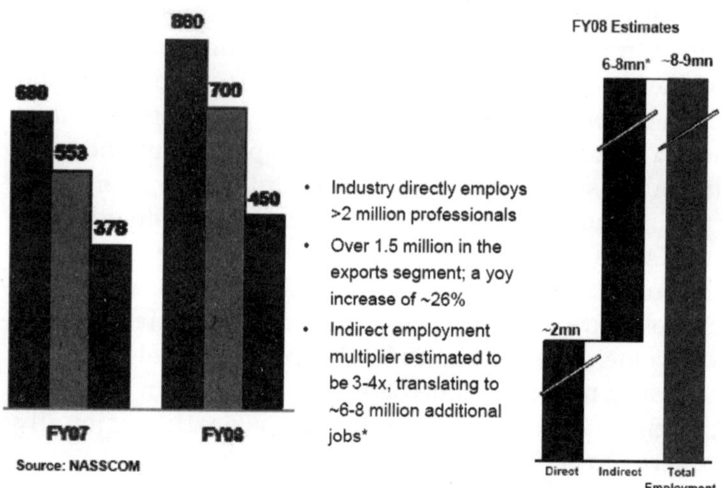

Fig. 9.4. Employee Data of Wipro

The company announced the cuts as it reported an 11% drop in second quarter profit, which fell short of Wall-streets expectations.

The job cuts will reduce the operating costs by $1.5bn as it prepares for lower revenue and earnings in the second half of the year.

Effects on Google

The search giant Google Inc., is cutting its recruiting staffs by 100 people as the company has slowed hiring due to bleak economic conditions. The recruitment staff reduction comes after Google stopped using many of its outside contractors, including those that provided recruiting services.

POSITIVE IMPACTS OF CRISIS ON JOB MARKET

Jobs up for Grabs in Medical Transcription

While job cuts have become a norm across industries, there

is one field which is looking for talent medical transcription (MT). Bucking the global trend, there are jobs up for grabs in this segment. Bangaluru, Hyderabad and Delhi are the main hubs for MT companies. Major companies in this field are positive about hiring.

Hiring Outlook for 2009

Companies across sectors are planning to hire more than 2,50,000 new employee over the next few months. This includes more than one lakh full time employees and about 1.5 lakh part time employees with insurance companies. While most of the hiring would take place in financial services industries, the over all job market scenario expected to recover in the second half of the year. Public sector banking giants like state bank Of India and PNB as well as insurance firms such as Reliance Life, SBI Life, MetLife, Max New York life will hire big. Also some BPOs and healthcare firms like ACS and Accentia are planning to hire thousands of people in coming months.

NEGATIVE IMPACTS

US Job Market Remains Grim

The US economy lost 2.6 million jobs in 2008, the highest decline since 1945 (2.75). The jobless rate at 7.2 per cent has been the highest since January 1993. Non-farm payrolls plunged by 524k in December, the 12th decline in a row. Of these, nearly two million job losses were in the last 4 months alone. The job losses were broad based across manufacturing, construction and most service industries.

2009 will Become a Tough Year for First Time Job Seekers

The India growth story has lost its sheen. This will clearly reflect on the job prospects of entry level job seekers this year. Job growth has slowed and many companies are optimizing their surplus staff and have frozen hiring. Campus recruitment has also down from the previous year. The big four giants TCS, Wipro, and Satyam are hiring less than last year

New Horizons for Indian Employees

Firstly, most of the IT firms are focusing on hiring limited fresher for their new long-term projects in Africa, Russia & East Asian countries through common wealth connects programmes.

Secondly, banks like CITI and HSBC are not cutting the jobs for their branches in India. Again, Standard Chartered, a financial institution, is focusing to hire more relationship managers by expanding its functions in consumer banking.

Thirdly, TCS is going to establish its delivery centres at Chennai, IBM has planned to establish "smart business centres" in India for the growth of small and medium scale enterprises.

SUGGESTIONS : (STEPS TAKEN BY INDIAN GOVERNMENT)

India takes various majors to overcome the crisis. Employment and income should a central focus to the fiscal stimulus packages :

- Give priority to the public spending programmes that have high multiplier effect on employment.
- Spread public spending and job creation broadly (including education, health, pension system).
- Target credit–constrained businesses (including SMEs) and consumers (the poor and low income households).

MAJOR FINDINGS AND CONCLUSION

Employee retention is the call of the day and is a first emerging area for human resource management, to develop the knowledge, skills aptitude and values of the employees so that they can perform the present and future job more effectively. Global financial crisis affects our banking and financial market. It affects both capital as well as stock market. Basically it has a great impact on service sector particularly on IT sector. Companies on IT an d financial sector continue the down size and cut costs and will not likely hire more people. It also affects the urban as well as the rural employment This crisis not only has the the negative impact on employment in IT, banking and other sectors but also it provided ample of opportunities in BPOs and health care units.

REFERENCES

Business Line, Bhubaneswar, October 6 2008.

Business Today, February 2009.

Badami S., (2008), *"Sub Prime Mortage Crisis",* The Management Accountant, August, pp. 571-575.

Ckliu Hery, (2007). *"Liquidity Crisis Looming Boom",* Asia Times, May 09, 2009.

Frontline, Volume- 26, Issue-05, 13 March 2009, pp. 33-34.

Mukopadhya D., (2008). *"US Subprime Lending Crisis & Warning for India",* The Management Accountant, August, pp. 568-570.

The Analyst, Volume XV, Issue-03, March 2009, pp. 19, 74-76.

The Economics Time, Kolkata, April 09 & 14, 2009.

CHAPTER

Curse of Global Recession on Employment in India

Minati Sahoo
Kabita Kumari Sahu

Recession refers to the state of economy when it is having a negative growth rate. This dragon recession has taken in its tight grip to most of the nations of the world, some of whom are suffering abysmally even today. It all started when the financial institution named Merrill Lynch of US went bankrupt due to sub-prime crisis. And this was followed by the collapse of Goldman Sach and suddenly much other such institution lost their existence which had to be bailout. The whole of these events had such a great adverse and indirect impact not only in US but many of other world countries, which include India. India's GDP growth depend a lot on the FDI (foreign directive investment), FII (foreign institutional investor) and foreign investment in India. What actually happened after the giant Merrill and other institutions collapse that their clients and FII, FDI drew out money from the Indian stock market as a result BSE sensex dropped sharply from around 23000 base points to as low as 8000. People who had invested huge amounts in the stock market lost their considerable assets. Some of which couldn't bear the trauma and ended their life. Nobody could do anything to help somebody's out here. Government felt helpless to circumvent their pain. Government revenue generation through various sources also took a hit due to this sudden tragic events. Foreign exchange too was lowered. The IMF, World Economic Outlook (October 2008) describes the crisis as "the most dangerous financial shock in mature financial markets since the 1930s". This crisis is not an accidental; it is a systemic crisis of the capitalism in the area of globalisation and a free market which is linked to the huge accumulation of finance capital.

Impact of Recession on Employment

A report of the PTI stated that with every one minute ticking, companies across the world are terminating on an average five people. The statistics of unemployment in the U.S. - the epicentre of the crisis - are always revised and every time in only one way-upwards. In a single month of February, 2009, more than 6,94,000 jobs were lost in the US alone. Many a pathetic stories are coming from abroad. This is especially true for those who had gone to the Gulf and are forced to return as they are no longer required there. According to the Central Government, about 20,000 Indians have returned home after losing their jobs overseas due to global economic crisis. A U.S. study indicates that 100,000 Indians will return from U.S. in the next three years. The International Labour Organisation (ILO) found that global unemployment rise by more than 50 million and leave more than seven per cent of World's labour force without a job by the end of 2009. No wonder, close to 10 million jobs were lost during 2008. A whopping 85,000 job cuts were announced on a single day on January 26, 2009 alone.

The impact of global slowdown on India's economy is quite visible in the employment scenario in India. In fact the rising joblessness in India has assumed worrisome proportions. With overall economic growth sharply slowing down, the ranks of those without work are growing by the day. Five hundred thousand people were rendered jobless between October and December 2008, according to a first of its kind survey conducted by the Ministry of Labour and

Employment. With the global slump, the fortunes of those who work in the export industry have become equally bleak. India could lose up to 1.5 million jobs in this sector in the six months to March 2009. The Labour Ministry's numbers are based on a survey of 2,581 units covering 20 centres across 11 States. Eight major sectors like the textiles and garment industry, metals and metal products, information technology and business process outsourcing, automobiles, gems and jewellery, transportation, construction and mining industries were included. The total employment in these sectors had come down from 16.2 million in September 2008 to 15.7 million by December 2008 due to the Reword stalking Indian industry.

India's exports, too, have been contracting every month since October 2008 due to falling demand in the U.S. and Europe. Many units have downed their shutters and lay off staff. If these projections continue, it is quite likely that one can expect another 500,000 job losses before March 31, stated G.K. Pillai, Commerce Secretary, after announcing earlier that one million jobs had gone since August, 2008. Interestingly, more uptodate economy wide estimates of unemployment - based on extrapolations from recent trends - are consistent with the above numbers for job losses this year as growth is likely to decline to seven per cent as compared to 8.8 per cent per annum during the last five years. But with India's growth expected to plunge to five per cent next year, the incidence of joblessness will be more severe than before.

A disturbing trend of India's economic performance is a deceleration in employment growth to 1.92 per cent per annum from 1993-94 to 2006-07 from 2.61 per cent. Between 1983-1984 to 1993-94 although growth in terms of gross domestic product (GDP) was rapid. Clearly, there has been a decline in employment per unit of GDP growth or employment elasticity to 0.28 from 1993-94 to 2006-07 from 0.52 over the years 1983-1993-94. Applying this elasticity to the likely GDP growth of seven per cent in 2008-09 and five per cent in 2009-10 to project the generation of employment provides an average of eight million work opportunities this year and six million the next. This is much short of the 10 million opportunities generated during each of the past five years. In other words, there will be two million fewer jobs than before this year and four million fewer jobs next year. Besides this, the recession is bound to affect demand, capacity utilisation and employment in a wide range of manufacturing industries catering to the domestic market. Moreover, growth in a number of areas such as the housing sector, automobiles and consumer durables had been driven by credit financed purchases encouraged by easy liquidity and low interest rates. The curtailment of credit provision by a damaged or cautious financial sector would further reduce demand, increase inventories and lead to job losses in industries directly or indirectly catering to such credit-financed investment and consumption. Influence by these trends and the second order of effect of contraction in these areas on demand for other manufacturing sectors, there will be a wider range of industries and segments of the labour markets that will be affected by the ongoing crisis. Finally as a result of all these development, the demand for agricultural commodities and the viability of crop production is being increasingly eroded. The change in employment is shown below in Table 10.1.

Table 10.1. Percentage Change in Employment of Exporting and Non-exporting Units

Period	Exporting Units	Non-Exporting Units	Overall
October, 2008	–1.3	–1.05	–1.21
November, 2008	–0.45	–1.24	–0.74
December, 2008	–1.66	–0.15	–1.12
Average Monthly Change	–1.13	–0.81	–1.01

Source: Labour Bureau, Ministry of Labour and Employment

Unemployment in India's industrial and services sectors is on the rise. If earlier growth was being described as "jobless", the problem now is that growth that is lower comes with job losses. The recessionary impact that the global financial and economic crisis has had is resulting in huge job losses in various segments of the labour market. However, a reliable aggregate estimate of the extent of increase in unemployment is not available from the official statistical system. Recognizing that unemployment is on the rise, the government did make an attempt to estimate the impact of the downturn on employment. on its request, the Labour Bureau conducted a sample survey covering eight sectors (mining, textile & textile garments, gems & jewellery, construction, transport and IT/BPO industry) to arrive at an estimate of job loss. The survey was designed to cover a sample of units employing 10 or more workers, with the sample being drawn from 20 centres in 11 states and union territories.

Finally, 2581 units were covered , of which 1168 were from the textile & garments industry, 752 from metals & metal products, 242 from information technology & business process outsourcing, 132 from automobiles, 104 from gems & jewellery, 103 from transportation, 19 from mining, and 61 from construction. Based on this limited sample, the total employment in all the sectors covered by the survey is estimated to have declined from 16.2 million during December 2008, implying a job loss of about half a million. (Table 10.2) Given the coverage and methodology of the survey, few believe that this is an acceptable estimate. The actual decline in employment during this period is likely to have been much higher. Moreover, the decline is likely to have occurred over a much longer period.

However, the survey does suggest that employment fell in every month during the period studied. After September 2008 employment in all industry declined at an average rate of 1.01 per cent per month. A comparison of employment in export and non-export units indicates that employment declined at an average monthly rate of 1.13 per cent in the case of the former, as opposed to 0.81 per cent in the latter pointing to the direct role of the global slowdown. The trend in average employment is given below in table 10.2.

Table 10.2. Trends in Average Employment, India (In Million)

Period	Average Employment	%age Change
October, 08	16.2	–1.21
November, 08	16	–0.74
December, 08	15.9	–1.12
Average Monthly Change	15.7	–1.01

Source: Labour Bureau, Ministry of Labour and Employment.

Blue Collar Workers Ignored

With aggregate date being limited, the assessment of and response to rising unemployment has been driven by episodic evidence of job loss highlighted by the media. However, given the nature of India's boom and the pattern of recent growth it is the loss of white collar jobs that garners attention from the media. This was evident when Jet Airways, beleaguered by high oil prices, increased competition and falling demand, lay off around a thousand employees. The response to the announcement was so adverse that the company was forced to go back on its operations and obtaining concessions from the government to reduce its losses. Similarly, other labour market developments that have received and are receiving media attention are evidence of sluggishness in on-campus recruitment from elite institutions like the IITs and IIMs, lay-offs and redundancies in software services and business process outsourcing firms and evidence of job losses in Gulf countries. Much less attention has been paid to job losses of informally employed blue collar workers in the organised sector or those dependent on wage- or self-employment in unorganized manufacturing, services and agriculture.

Job Loss Depression

Job loss depression occurs when someone loses their employment. It can have long-lasting effects on the individual, sometimes lasting as long as two years. Job loss depression is not solely caused by the single event of losing one's job. The loss of employment can trigger a series of events, called a "cascade of negative life events". The loss of employment almost always means financial stress will follow. The longer one is unemployed the more financial difficulties one may experience. In addition, one may have lost health care benefits. In addition to the financial and relational strain that job loss causes, individuals usually suffer from feelings of insecurity, inferiority, and suffer from low self-esteem. They also may suffer from feelings of uncertainty about their current and future job stability. These feelings, associated with job loss depression, can last up to two years even if they have become gainfully employed. In addition to the emotional impact of job loss depression, studies have proven job loss depression worsen physical health also. During recession people are afflicted with a condition called the psychological recession. It is an emotional state in which people feel extremely vulnerable and afraid for their futures. It is especially relevant in the business world because chronically fearful people are too exhausted to be creative and innovative. They expect the worst to happen, so they see no reason to give their all. The psychological downturn, especially when combined with the current economic recession, is far worse than the 2001 economic slowdown, and its cause is not explained by outside factors like media bias. This sense of pessimism is rooted in the profound and sustained feelings of vulnerability that many people are experiencing. Anxiety, depression, and a sense of being powerless are a poisonous mix. The impact of a psychological recession is more widespread than most people realise because nearly everyone personally knows people who have been directly affected. The result is that even those who are still working are anxious and fearful. They watch their former colleagues, especially the "golden ones", struggle through months or even years of unemployment. They see their companies continuing to downsize, use temps, and outsource, and they're afraid they may be next. Stress is everywhere, and it is unrelenting.

At the same time, work itself has become a major source of tension, because when costs must be lowered, the arithmetic of higher productivity means that more work has to be accomplished by fewer and fewer people. This translates to longer work hours for everyone who has a job. But it's not simply a question of overwork, of too many hours. When people are anxious at work, they're afraid that no amount of effort is good enough. To make themselves safe, they work very hard at everything. They don't feel secure enough, and therefore are not courageous enough, to differentiate among tasks and set priorities. When every task is treated as enormously important, work never ends. There's no closure, no sense of satisfaction of a job well done. People on permanent overload are exhausted, and exhaustion is not a prescription for treating fear and anxiety.

Suggestion to Lessen Adverse Impacts of Recession

The obvious panacea for the crisis is the injection of demand in to the system through public expenditure; injection of liquidity alone is not enough, since both financial institution and individual wealth holders simply absorb all such injected liquidity, without stimulating private demand via easier credit. To protect ourselves from the global crisis, we have to increase aggregate demand. Aggregate demand can be enhanced by creating jobs and putting purchasing power in the hands of under privileged people who tend to have a higher propensity consume. These will not only make the growth process more sustainable but also more inclusive and equitable. Massive dose of public investment is the only way to stimulate growth. Governments must inject demand into the real economy directly not just liquidity. Some steps, governments must take to protect ourselves these are as follows :

- Strengthen our real economy by increasing public investment.
- Ensure bank credit to farmers and weaker sections.
- Stabilize the Indian rupee.
- Stop relaxing measures for capital inflows.
- Stop efforts to deregulate and opening up banking and insurance sector.
- Reverse capital account convertibility.
- Prohibit participatory notes.
- Strictly regulate securitized debt.

Recovery in Sight

After recession can be referred as the second life and second opportunity for many, as it caused worldwide unemployment records, lay-offs, and financial problems for most people. Some economic analyst and experts said that the worldwide economic recovery is real and our financial positions will be stabilised. They are also constantly speculating about the scenarios that could develop once the world moved out of the recession. The dent in consumer confidence in the last survey was attributed to the uncertainty in the jobs market, the unavailability of consumer finance and the depressed state of the stock markets. The latest round of the Nielsen Global Consumer Confidence Survey reveals a sharp increase in confidence levels, Indians being the second most optimistic. After slipping from 114 in September 2008 to 99 in March 2009, India's consumer confidence index has risen to 112 in June.

In the past few months, workplace retrenchments have by and large stopped. In anticipation of an economic recovery soon, several companies have lifted the freeze on recruitment and begun to hire people. Most companies feel that this is a good time to hire because salary expectations are still modest. At the same time, the liquidity crisis has eased. Led by public sector banks, the availability of home and car loans has improved vastly. Car makers have recorded strong growth in sales in June and July 2009. The rapid recovery in Surat, India's diamond manufacturing centre, and in Mumbai, its trading hub, reflects factors far beyond the opportunism of its mainstay companies. Most attribute the minimal effect the recession had there on two factors that were lacking in other markets: the organized response of the Indian industry and the strength of the domestic market for jewellery.

India added 487,000 jobs in its IT and BPO (business process outsourcing) export industries in the quarter ended Dec. 31, 2009 despite the global recession, according to a Quarterly Quick Employment Survey by the country's labour bureau. The results found that of a total of 638,000 jobs added across the economy, 580,000 were in the exports sector. IT services and BPO exporters led the pack.TCS, for example, added 7,692 positions in last quarter of 2009, taking the total staff at the end of the quarter to 149,654. The company plans to hire about 8,000 trainees and about 3,000 experienced staff in the current quarter, it said. So our economy is reviving.

Conclusion

This global crisis needs a global solution and preventing an economic catastrophe in developing countries is important for global efforts to overcome this crisis. "We need to react in real time to a growing crisis that is hurting people in developing countries," said World Bank Group President Robert B. Zoellick. Before the start of financial crisis and then the economic recession, the world was consistently moving towards technology and the use of processes that saved the labour costs. We're in globalization of productive activities and an economy that exploited the brain rather than the force in people. Our vision in work is about a man versus a machine, a worker in one part of the world against another worker in another part of the world and a worker in white collar using a computer versus a man in blue collar with a hammer. Could this scenario will change and the trends can be reverse? Do people will get a job after this recession? People are afraid for this question as they know that many people lost their jobs, chances, opportunities and still hoping for the second possibility. The old-fashioned way in finding a job on the other hand, can still work and use to start once again. We should learn to embrace new things and be open for new challenges. It is believed that the development and changes that we've learned from this recession will gave us opportunities, challenges and well living.

REFERENCES

Bose, Prasenjit (2008) "Current Crisis on Global capitalism", *Student Struggle*.

Chandrasekhar, C.P. (2009) "Current Capitalist Crisis", *People's Democracy*.

Economic Survey, Government of India.

Mitra, Ashok (2008) "Global Economic Crisis", *Student struggle*, Nov. 2009.

National Conference On "GLOBAL MELTDOWN-Issues, challenges & strategies" at Institute of Management & Technology, Faridabad

Patnaik, Pravat (2009) "Neo-Liberalism on the brink of failure", *People's Democracy*.

Reddy, Y. V. (1009): India And The Global Financial Crisis.

CHAPTER

Series of Lay-off Impact Across World : Role of HR Manager Surviving in such Economy

Sthitaprajna Debadutta Samal

ABSTRACT

Most of the countries all over the world are going through this phase of economic recession. Many old and big companies have already been brought down on their knees to bite the dust. Many companies as well as countries have become bankrupt or are on the verge of it. Millions and millions of people have lost their jobs. Many people have lost millions and billions of dollars. People in general are scared and fearsome. This is not the first time that the global economy is going through recession and this is also not the last time. There is a pattern involved in it. On an average it is happening after every 8-10 years. It's easy to view a layoff as an end-of-the-world situation. Few experiences are scarier than losing your job and the financial security it brings. The fear and desperation that grip you after you've been laid off are destructive emotions. They distract from doing the work need to do to find a new job.

Lay-off, Downsizing, Cost Cutting, Cutbacks and Lean Methodologies giggles around us in today's economic environment. The global economic downturn finally hit IT industries by routinely filling the headlines with the layoff announcements and unemployment numbers rising. However, the term can also refer to the permanent elimination of a position in an organisation. This article critically attempts to review literatures in the areas of Layoff and attempts to throw light on HR Policies and Procedures for surviving a layoff in a down economy.

KEY WORDS

Layoff, Economic Recession, Downsizing, Cost Cutting.

INTRODUCTION

Lay-off is the temporary suspension or permanent termination of employment of an employee a group of employees for business reasons, such as the decision that certain positions are no longer necessary or a business slow-down or interruption in work. Originally the term "lay-off" referred exclusively to a temporary interruption in work, as when factory work cyclically falls-off.

Companies discover that the only way to survive is to dramatically cut back, often that includes lean the resource size. It's the classic layoff problem. Relief from bottom-line, pressure on the one hand; and low morale, bad publicity, and the loss of talented employees on the other hand. The economy is entering a two-layoff cycle. Managements examined their 2009 prospects late last year and prepared layoffs based on their knowledge that the current year would be rough. They made their job reductions based on those assumptions. But, many executives were completely wrong about the length and severity of this recession. It is hard to blame them for this mistake. Even well-regarded economists have had trouble giving reasonable forecasts for what will happen to joblessness, consumer spending, and industrial production over the next two or three months.

The method of separation may have an effect on a former employee's ability to collect whatever form of unemployment compensation might be available in their jurisdiction.

In the U.S. many workers who are laid-off can file an unemployment claim and receive compensation. Depending on local or State laws, workers who leave voluntarily are generally ineligible to collect unemployment benefits, as are those who are fired for gross misconduct. Also, lay-offs due to a firm's moving production overseas may entitle one to increased re-training benefits.

REVIEW OF LITERATURE

09 Jan 2009 : Latest news is coming that Satyam is thinking to layoff arround 10000 employee till Feb. 2009. There is no salary for another two months.

According to Times of India

Satyam Computers, which has just started giving pink slips to its employees, could potentially downsize its workforce by a whopping 4,500 employees. This translates to a little less than 9 per cent of the 51,000 employees that the company employs.

Company sources say 1,500 employees have been put under the performance improvement plan (PIP), euphemism for employees put on watch list and asked to shape up or ship out. Apart from this, 3,000 others have not been given any increment in the last appraisal cycle, thereby indicating that their services are dispensable.

India's Tata Consultancy to Lay Off 1,300 Staffs

Business News, March 8, 2009.

India's largest software company, Tata Consultancy Services (TCS), will lay-off 1300 of its employees over the next few months, the *Times of India* newspaper reported Sunday. Those made redundant will be staff who fail to meet performance standards, it said. The redundancies represent around one per cent of its 130,000-strong global workforce, the Times of India daily reported, citing company officials. "This is mostly employees who have been given a second chance to improve and haven't. They will be sent over a period, in the next few months. We had to let go of 500 people last year on performance issues," a TCS spokesman told the newspaper. The report did not specify countries where the job cuts would be made. The TCS serves over 800 clients in 42 countries.

Indian IT companies are adopting stringent appraisal, cost-trimming and productivity-boosting measures as they deal with the global economic slowdown.

The firms are particularly worried about the crisis in the US since a bulk of their business comes from that country's financial sector.

The TCS employees told the Times that the layoffs have already started at the company's development centres in southern Chennai city, where over 200 employees have been asked to leave in the last fortnight.

The TCS, part of one of India's largest and oldest conglomerates, the Tata Group, recorded worldwide annual sales of 5.7 billion dollars for the fiscal year ending March, 2008.

Minimal Jobs Cuts in Sun Microsystems India, to Focus on PSUs

Sutanuka Ghosal, ET Bureau, KOLKATA (16 Jan 2009)

Santa Clara-based $13.88 billion Sun Microsystems will lay off staff in India as part of its plan to cut 6000 jobs globally. The company employs some 33,423 people worldwide. While the company is yet to decide the exact number of job cuts in India, it has no plans for fresh hiring in 2009.

The company, which operates in more than 100 countries around the globe, employs some 1300 people in India. "The number of job cuts in India will be minimal as the country is projected as one of the emerging markets along with Brazil, Russia and China. Fresh hiring will hardly be there.

IBM Land off ~700 Employees (Mostly Freshers)

Indian firms are likely to lay off a quarter of their employees in the next 10 days, as part of steps to contain costs in the face of shrinking margins amidst the economic turmoil, an industry body said on Wednesday. Trade body Associated Chambers of Commerce and Industry of India (ASSOCHAM) said the job cuts would be across the steel, cement, construction, real estate, aviation, IT-enabled services and financial services sectors.

Expansion has slowed in *Asia's third-largest economy in* the last two quarters, from the eight per cent or more annual growth in the past four years, with high interest rates crimping demand and on the global financial crisis.

The Central Bank last week cut its forecast for growth in 2008/09 to 7.5-8 per cent from its earlier view of eight per cent. This compares with the economy's nine per cent growth in 2007-08.

> "Employers have no other alternatives as part of their corporate strategy for sustaining their operations with squeezed margins (even) after after drastic cost cutting measures," ASSOCHAM said in a statement.

Objectives of the Study

The objectives of this study are :

1. To study the Global Economic Recessions situations.
2. To study the concept of Lay-off in this present dynamic era.
3. To provide the information on companies affecting on such acute problem of an economy.
4. And what should be remedial measures(HR Policies) to be taken to solve such problem?

Research Methodology

The data of this study have been collected through secondary sources like :

1. Newspapers.
2. Magazines.

3. Journals.
4. And other research publications of eminent scholars.

Secrets for Surviving Lay-off in a Down Economy

It's easy to view a layoff as an end-of-the-world situation. Few experiences are scarier than losing your job and the financial security it brings. The fear and desperation that grip you after you've been laid off are destructive emotions. They distract you from doing the work you need to do to find a new job.

Dr. Richard Bayer, a former professor of economics and ethics providing seven secrets for surviving in a Down Economy. The key, says Bayer, is maintaining a positive attitude because potential employers can detect a candidate's desperation as easily as a shark can smell blood, and they don't like it. To keep a stiff upper lip, Bayer offers the following seven tips for thriving after a layoff, even in a bad economy.

Strategies to Avoid the Lay-off

1. **Cautious Hiring Strategy :** Hiring appropriately leads to escape of lay offs. When you can afford more hired hands, should not step into overboard. Bottom line the starting salary for an employee based on what you have.

   So that, when work slows to crawl, workers and your company won't be overloaded in overhead.

2. **Employee-Exchange Strategy :** Employees can be placed in temporary jobs with other companies for a set period, usually not longer than six weeks, during slowdowns. This program allows providing improved job stability. Though might reduce the payroll when necessary, but to still have trained workers available when needed.

3. **Shared Work Strategy :** Shared Work is a voluntary program that provides employers facing a temporary

decline in business. Rather than laying off a percentage of the work force to cut costs, an employer can reduce the hours and wages of all or a particular group of employees.

4. **Corporate Welfare Strategy :** Corporate Welfare deals with cutting down the several percentage of monthly pay and saves towards future. When economic heads down, avoid laying off by utilizing corporate welfare funds as employee's monthly salary.

   If no layoffs, pay back the savings when employee quits the company.

5. **Future Force :** Encourage domain based R&D group in your company. Get all the high profiled benched employees to R&D group based on their domain expertise and their interest. R & D Technology group foresees the future technologies to satisfy an ever growing market demand.

6. **Patenting Ideas :** The role of patents in technology market is huge. Anyone can be innovative if they put their mind to it. It may not happen overnight; anyone can become an inventor ! So tune up your employees to solve your own company's problem and use a little bit of innovation. If you can come up with a solution for those problems and get a patent on your idea, you will be the one to capitalize on it.

7. **Trim down the perks :** Before you take the knife to regular benefits, take a hard look at office extras. Perks should be the first thing to go, unless employee morale is going to plummet. Skipping a year-end bonus can save your company money. If it's a question of getting a bonus and getting a pink slip, most employees will thankfully skip the extra pay if it ensures their long-term employment.

8. **Early-out Options :** Companies also can save jobs by offering severance to senior employees who are

close to retirement. That's how a majority of human resource professionals surveyed by the Society for Human Resource Management said they were cutting back without laying off workers.

9. **Salary Cuts :** People understand company is in a very extraordinary set of circumstances, and extraordinary times require extraordinary measures. Taking a pay cut is preferable to losing your job. Depending on the company's business status, certain percentage of pay cuts can be announced.
10. **Limits offices :** If your company has remote offices, consider closing them and sending your employees home to work. In today's world, most of the companies has facility work from home. Employee's prefer it that way, and it saves the company money on real estate.
11. **Increase Your Businesses :** During Market slowdown, businesses would gradually reduce and the number of staff (resources) would increase. The problem isn't that you have too many staff for the business you have, but too little business for the staff you have. Puts a different perspective on the problem. This creates an imbalance between the amount of business and the number of staff. To set this balance, Companies should bring in more businesses.

This could be done by training the benched employees in presales of their domain in the market and encourage more sales or service. Thereby bringing in more businesses, which would set the balance of business and staff.

Pattern

There is a set process that needs to be followed at the time of laying-off. I am not sure how many companies actually follow it. Let me elaborate :

1. Freezing the recruitment. No new hiring.
2. Fresh graduates or those who are new to the market will find it difficult to get a job. More so, if they are not from A-grade institutes.

3. Last in, First Out. Among the employees who are already inside the company and are employed, the person who has joined recently will be the first one to go out. To be more precise, all those who are on their probation will be shown the door.
4. Average performers or difficult employee will also be shown the door. Performance records of last three years will be re-examined and reanalyzed and those with average or below average performance will be shown the door.
5. Outsourcing to increase. Most of the routine functions will be outsourced and those departments will be closed.

What More to Expect?

1. Training and Development programs to freeze. No more expenditures on company sponsored training and development programs.
2. Perks, benefits and retention allowances to be withdrawn. The company will freeze all perks and benefits that has been extended to its senior employees.
3. Bonuses and incentives to be stopped. For the time being the companies will stop all the bonuses and incentives that are due to its employees.
4. Specialists are out and generalists are in. At the time when economy was booming, companies might have hired different people for different role within a function/department or most likely they have hired more than one person for a role, all these arrangements will go away and only those people who are willing to do the work of more than one person or those who can do multiple roles will stay in.

This is the basic process that is followed in many companies at the time of such economic crisis. What does it means to the people in general and what they should be doing? There is something to be learned from every crisis and this one is no different.

Learnings

It is not important to know what is happening across the world but it is important to know what is happening in your company. It is also important to keep an eye on the market situation and keep yourself updated with the latest. If you are the one who has been laid-off, then you must be the one falling in any of the above mentioned scenarios.

I think you also need to take the blame of your current situation. However, there is no need to get panic. Hold your emotions and look around.

If you are the one who has been laid-off then you must do the following :

1. Time with family. Remember when you were working and working for 12-15 hours a day, how difficult it was for you to find some time for your family. Now is your time to be with your family. Spend some time with them. Strengthen your bond with them.
2. Improve your skills and personality. No one is perfect and there is a scope for improvement in everyone of us. Use this time to work on your areas of improvement and weaknesses. Sharpen your skills.
3. Work on your professional and personal network. Networking is very important for the growth of an individual. Use this time to build and strengthen your professional and personal network, so that whenever the market situation improves, you get the benefit of it.

Heading back to schools, colleges and institutes. This is also a good time for you to share your knowledge and experiences with new generation and to pass on your intellectual legacy to them. Get associated with some colleges and institutes to do so. There is a possibility that you might get paid for it, which in turn might give you the required financial support.

Conclusion

To conclude it can be said that Layoff, Downsizing, Cost Cutting, Cutbacks and Lean Methodologies giggles around us in today's economic environment. The global economic downturn finally hit IT industries by routinely filling the headlines with the lay off announcements and unemployment numbers rising in different MNC's also. So here Companies discover that the way to survive from such problem. In the mean time HR persons having crucial role to handle such circumstances through the above discussed methods.

REFERENCES

Business News, March 8, 2009, 11:40 GMT.

Rao, V.S.P. (2008), Separation, Layoff and solutions to solve it, Methods.

Rao, Subba, (2006), Separation and its types.

Yojana, State of Economy, March, June, July, Aug-2009.

CHAPTER

International Financial Crisis and its Impact on Indian Economy : An Assessment

A. Abdul Raheem

ABSTRACT

The international financial crisis originated in the sub-prime mortgage crisis which surfaced nearly two years ago in the U.S. With interest rates rising and home prices falling, there was a sharp jump in defaults and foreclosures. However, this would have remained as a purely mortgage market crisis but for the fact that these sub-prime mortgages were securitized and packaged into products that were rated as investment grade. Once doubts about these assets arose they turned illiquid; it also became very hard to price them. As a result, it started affecting a host of institutions which had invested in these products. These institutions were not confined to US alone. Financial institutions in Europe and to a much lesser extent in East Asia had such assets on their books. With the failure of a few leading institutions and most notably Lehman Brothers, the entire financial system was enveloped into an acute crisis. There was mutual distrust among the financial institutions which led to freezing up of several markets including the overnight inter-bank market. Many think today that letting the Lehman Brothers to fail was a great mistake. The crisis in the financial system has now moved to affect the real sector in a significant way. Therefore, this paper identifies global financial crisis and its impact on Indian economy.

INTRODUCTION

The crisis which began with the bursting of the housing bubble in the U.S. and high incidence of default s on sub-prime mortgages early last year has its origins in the loose monetary policy followed under former Chairman of the U.S. Federal Reserve, Alan Greenspan. In a bid to counter the economic slowdown brought on by the dotcom bust of 2000, the US Fed steadfastly lowered interest rates to one per cent during the period till 2004 before raising it to 5.25 per cent in 2006. The combination of rising prosperity and low interest rates led to a sharp increase in demand for housing loans even as easy liquidity saw a run up in all asset values, including houses. This encouraged borrowers to assume expensive mortgages in the belief that they would be able to get refinance on more favourable terms. However, once interest rates began to rise and housing prices started to drop in many parts of the U.S. in 2006-07, refinancing became more difficult. Defaults and foreclosures became commonplace once home prices stopped going up and then started falling. What made matters worse was that banks and mortgage lenders that had securitised their loans by issuing mortgage-backed securities, based on underlying mortgage payments, suddenly found the value of these securities falling rapidly as defaults rose. Major banks and financial institutions, both in the U.S. and in many other developed countries, that had borrowed and invested hugely in such securities lost heavily. Credit default swaps that were meant to act as insurance against the risk that borrowers will not pay back bank loans and make the financial system less risky (because they allow holders of securitised instruments to offset the risk of holding them) failed to provide the expected comfort. The fear now is that CDS issuers may not be able to fulfill their obligations in case of a default in which case there is a very real danger of the credit crisis worsening. The first hint of trouble came from the collapse of two Bear Stearns hedge funds early last. Subsequently a number of other banks and financial institutions also began to show signs of distress. However, matters really came to a head with the bankruptcy of Lehman Brothers, an iconic investment bank, in September 2008.

The U.S. government's failure to rescue Lehman destroyed what little confidence there was among market participants. As inter-bank lending seized up and banks refused to lend each other, funds flow to the larger economy became constrained. Stock markets across the world plummeted on account of rising risk aversion and the resultant flight to safety. Faced with the fear of productive sectors of the economy being denied credit, central banks and governments around the world announced various economic stimulus packages to spur growth and instill confidence in financial markets. These moves have as yet had limited impact in ameliorating the distress. The meeting in Washington of the heads of state of the G20 on 15 November is the latest attempt at coordinated policy action to stave off what many regard as the most serious economic crisis since the Great Depression of the 1930s.

IMPACT OF THE CRISIS ON BASIC ECONOMIC FUNDAMENTALS

Economic Growth

The impact of the financial crisis is being felt on the growth of the major economies of the world and, in turn, on global commodity prices. The International Monetary Fund (IMF) expects advanced economies to contract 0.3 per cent on a full-year basis next year. In its November 2008 revision of its World Economic Outlook 2008 it has slashed its global growth forecast to 2.2 per cent, blaming the global credit crunch. Less than a month ago the IMF forecast growth of 0.5 per cent in the advanced economies and 3 per cent worldwide. As the epicenter of the crisis, the US is expected to experience a significant slowdown. According to the IMF the US economy will show positive growth for 2008, but at a tepid rate of 1.4 per cent, with the second-half contraction offsetting growth in the first six months of the year. Growth in the eurozone is forecast to shrink drastically by half a point in 2009, the IMF said, instead of the 0.2 percent growth seen in its October Outlook.

Inevitably, the slowdown of the major economies of the world has spilled over to economies like China and India thanks to their increasing integration into the world economy following the reforms of the 1980s and 1990s respectively. According to the IMF, China is expected to be relatively less impacted with its economy projected to grow at 9.7 and 8.5 per cent in 2008 and 2009 respectively, though this is lower than the average 11.5 per cent in previous years. India is estimated to grow at 7.8 and 6.3 per cent in 2008 and 2009 respectively as against its average growth rate of 8.7 per cent since 2003-04.

Price Situation

The credit crunch in the market has had a dampening effect on world commodity markets. The price of major commodities in the world has fallen steadily, due to sluggish demand. Consumers are apprehensive about spending more; at the same time, increased market volatility and the liquidity crunch have increased uncertainty. Table 12.1 shows world commodity prices during the past three months starting from October 2008. Prices of crude oil and natural gas fell by 45 and 39.3 per cent respectively between July and October while prices of vegetable oil like palm oil and coconut oil declined by 39.4 and 50 per cent respectively. Prices of essentials like rice and wheat also fell by 16.7 and 27.7 per cent respectively. In the metal groups copper and silver price fell over 40 per cent while gold and steel fell by 14.2 and 22.4 per cent respectively during the same period. The fall in commodity prices is bound to temper the inflationary pressure that the world was facing only few months earlier. Average consumer price index inflation is expected to come down from 4.2 per cent in 2008 to 1.8 per cent in 2009. However that is the only silver lining in an otherwise bleak scenario with most of the world economy already into a recession.

Table 10.1. Major Commodity Prices of World

Commodity		July	Aug	Sep	Oct	(Sep-Oct) Reduction (%)	(July-Oct) Reduction (%)
Crude oil, Brent	$/bbl	133.9	113.8	99.06	72.84	26.5	45.6
Natural gas US	$/mmbtu	11.1	8.3	7.69	6.73	12.4	39.3
Coconut oil	$/mt	1436	1188.8	1.104	870	21.2	39.4
Palm oil	$/mt	1128	884	760	564	25.8	50.0
Rice, Thailand, 5%	$/mt	731.8	693.5	686.3	603.3	11.2	16.7
Wheat, US, HRW	$/mt	328.2	329.3	294.5	237.4	19.4	27.7
Rubber, Singapore	C/kg	321.6	294.9	288.1	193.5	32.8	39.8
Aluminum	$/mt	3071.2	2764.4	2.526	2.121	16.0	30.9
Copper	$/mt	8414	7634.7	6.991	4.926	29.5	41.5
Gold	$ltoz	939.8	839	829.9	806.6	2.8	14.2
Iron ore	c/dmtu	140.6	140.6	140.6	140.6	6.0	0.0
Silver	cltoz	1806.4	1457.8	1.219	1.043	14.5	42.3
Steel	$/mt	980	1030	792.5	760.0	4.1	22.4

Source: World Bank Pink sheet.

Is this the 1929 Great Depression Revisited?

Many have compared the present crisis with the 1929 Great Depression and though there are undoubtedly similarities there are a number of differences as well that give us reason to hope the distress will not be on the scale witnessed in the 1930s. In both cases the epicenter is the U.S.A. and the proximate cause, indiscriminate borrowing and spending by US citizens, is also the same. The present credit crisis was caused by huge borrowing and spending on homes leading to inflated home values, while the crisis in 1929 was the outcome of increased spending (using borrowed money) on radios, cars and appliances. But there is a key difference. The present US economy is 20 per cent of the world economy; in 1929 it was only three per cent. The unemployment rate during 1929 was 5 per cent; it increased to 8.5 per cent in 1933 and further to 15 per cent 1940. However, the unemployment rate in the US is presently only 6.1 per cent and though it is expected to increase following the failure of several banks and financial institutions, the government has been far more proactive this time round. Policy makers have acted fast to offset the downward momentum with a series of dramatic steps: nationalising banks, guaranteeing deposits, increasing money supply, slashing interest rates. The present Chairman of the U.S. Federal Reserve Ben Bernanke, who has done extensive research on the Great Depression, has been at the forefront of formulating far more aggressive policy interventions together with the U.S. Treasury Secretary, Hank Paulson. The US Fed rate is down to 1 per cent, the Bank of England cut its policy rate by an unprecedented 1.5 pecentage points early November while the European Central Bank reduced interest rates by 50 basis points. Hence it is reasonable to expect that the U.S., and hence the world economy, will have a softer landing this time.

Regulatory Failure

What stands out glaringly in the current episode is the

regulatory failure. The regulatory failure was two-fold. *First*, some parts of the financial system were either loosely regulated or were not regulated at all, a factor which led to "regulatory arbitrage" with funds moving more towards the unregulated segments. The *second* failure lies in the imperfect understanding of the implications of various derivative products. In one sense, derivative products are a natural corollary of financial development. They meet a felt need. However, if the derivative products become too complex to discern where the risk lies, they become a major source of concern. Rating agencies in the present episode were irresponsible in creating a booming market in suspect derivative products. Quite clearly, there was a mismatch between financial innovation and the ability of the regulators to monitor them. It is ironic that such a regulatory failure should have occurred at a time when intense discussions were being held in Basle and elsewhere to put in place a sound regulatory framework.

Immediate Tasks

The immediate tasks before the authorities in the developed world are two-fold. *One* is to fix the financial system and *the other* is to maintain the aggregate demand at a high enough level to stimulate the real sector. Since it is the tail of the financial system that is wagging the dog of the economy, the first priority is to take care of the financial system and this is being done in a number of ways. Liquidity is being provided to key institutions which are locked into assets that cannot be easily realized. In the U.S., the Federal Reserve has lowered the policy rate to near zero. It has also injected liquidity in an abundant measure. Consequently, the balance sheet of the Federal Reserve has expanded from $900 billion to $2.2 trillion. The Troubled Assets Relief Programme of $700 billion approved by the U.S. Congress is being utilized to inject more capital into banks and other institutions. There was some doubt whether the package will be used to buy distressed assets. The recent Gaithner proposal has chalked out a programme to buy "toxic" assets. Some think that buying the assets is important because this will lead to revival of markets such as housing. To stimulate the economy, a massive revival package is being thought of in the U.S. This is a straight forward application of the Keynesian prescription. The U.S. Congress at the initiative of President Obama has passed a stimulus package of nearly $800 billion.

Medium Term Concerns

Even as these immediate tasks are addressed, there are medium term concerns. Many of the weaknesses of the financial system developed in an environment of very low interest rates. Pushing interest rates below a level that is not sustainable can also have its consequences. The U.S. has been incurring heavy current account deficits year after year for a decade or so. While analysts have been pointing out to the danger of such a situation, the authorities have been brushing aside these concerns by saying that the US was the desired destination for the investors. But the danger of such a situation is that once there is loss of confidence, it can have serious consequences. The U.S. must address this issue. A closely related to this is the issue is of leveraging. Almost every segment of the U.S. society including households is a net borrower. Many of the institutions that have fallen into trouble in the current episode are those which were highly leveraged. The net savings rate of the household sector stands negative. It is true that in a globalised system a country's investment rate is not solely determined by its savings rate. Nevertheless, the extent of leverage is an issue which regulators and policy-makers must pay attention, if financial stability is to be achieved.

International Co-ordination

The present crisis calls for coordinated efforts of all affected countries. *First*, a simultaneous effort at stimulating the economy will have a profound effect on aggregate demand. *Second*, the various countries must avoid protectionist policies.

This is a lesson that we have learnt from the depression of 1930s. *Third*, the international financial institutions need to strengthened in order to enable them to meet the financial needs of poor developing countries badly affected by the crisis. There are of course, some fundamental issues which need to be addressed with respect to the international financial institutions, such as ownership, voting power and management control.

IMPACT ON INDIA

The Indian financial system is not directly exposed to the "toxic" or "distressed" assets of the developed world. This is not surprising since Indian banks have very few branches abroad. However, the indirect impact on the economy because of the recession abroad is very much there. The "decoupling" theory does not hold good. The indirect impact is felt both through trade and capital flows. The fall in international commodity prices and more particularly crude oil is reducing sharply the import bill from previous estimates. The recession abroad is having an adverse effect on our exports of goods and services. There is a sharp deceleration in the rate of growth of exports in 2008-09. The decline in growth rate in exports will affect strongly some sectors where exports constitute a significant proportion of the total production. Some examples are textiles, automobile components and gem and jewellery. In contrast, to the strong inflow of over $100 billion last year, this year may not see any net increase in capital flows. Portfolio capital has already turned negative, with a significant impact on the stock market. Indian firms may also experience difficulties in raising money abroad. All this will impact the exchange rate.

Monetary and Fiscal Actions

The Indian financial system has not been affected in the same way the financial system abroad has been affected for reasons already explained. However, there is the impact of the drying up of liquidity because of the fall in reserves. The inability of Indian firms to raise funds abroad, including trade credit, puts pressure on the domestic banking system for more credit. It is, in this context, one must view the actions of the Reserve Bank of India in expanding liquidity. Reduction of the CRR and REPO and reverse REPO rates are steps in the right direction. It is necessary for the RBI to watch the liquidity situation and take such actions as are necessary from time to time. It is being pointed out that the actions of the RBI have not percolated to the ground level. People point to the slow growth in credit. Is this a case of "taking the horse to the pond but cannot compel it to drink?". The role of the Reserve Bank of India is to create an environment in which additional credit can be made available. Our fiscal actions to stimulate the economy have taken two forms. *One* is to cut excise duty and the *second* is to enlarge government expenditure. Both should lead to stimulating aggregate demand. It depends finally on whether the additional expenditures planned are actually incurred. Also we need to look at the composition of expenditure and effectiveness of expenditures. "Digging holes and filling them up" is not a right prescription. Expenditures should be biased towards investment so that capacities can be created which can facilitate growth later. That public spending should remain at a high level in a situation like the present one is not a matter for dispute. The revised estimates of total expenditure for 2008-09 are 20 per cent higher than the budget estimates. With this increase in expenditure, the fiscal deficit in the current year is estimated at six per cent of GDP, three percentage points above the FRBM target. While it is correct to argue that the fiscal deficit target should be an average over the cycle, we need to remember that even in boom years we have not been able to hold the deficit at the target level. Keeping the target as a cyclical average is a good guidance in the medium term. We should revert to the FRBM targets, as the economy begins to recover. As far as India is concerned, we will see signs of recovery in the second half of 2009.

Fiscal 2010-11 will see a distinct improvement in growth. It is contended by some that India "escaped" from a serious impact of the financial crisis because financial sector reforms were not pushed forward. This is a false assertion. The financial sector reforms in India are intended to improve the efficiency of the financial system. Had we pushed hard in this direction, it would not have had any adverse effect. The shock waves produced by the financial crisis will have their own effect on the structure of capitalism. Acceptable capitalism would require more regulation. Future discussions must centre around the nature and scope of such regulation. Run-a-way financial innovations that are dysfunctional do more harm than good. There are the lessons that we can draw from the current financial crisis.

CONCLUSION

The Indian economy has shown considerable resilience in the face of the present global financial crisis. The financial sector has emerged without much damage thanks in part to our strong regulatory framework and in part on account of state ownership of most of the banking sector. However, it would be naïve to expect the real economy to be completely unaffected by the global slowdown. The immediate impact of the crisis is the drying up of dollar liquidity as FIIs pull out their money from the stock market and sources of overseas credit and trade credit dry up. While large corporates will no doubt be affected, the worst affected are likely to be the exports and SMEs (small and marginal enterprises) that contrib ute significantly to employment generation. RBI's efforts to ease the downward pressure on the rupee (by selling dollars) have added to the domestic liquidity crunch in a scenario where corporates are increasingly turning to the domestic banking sector to make up for the drying up of external sources of finance and the IPO (initial public offering) market. Despite robust growth of 30 per cent in bank credit (year-on-year), corporates are complaining of a credit crunch. The only silver lining is the decline in inflation–latest numbers show inflation at 8.98 per cent for the week ended 1st November, 2008. Unfortunately, the scope for fiscal measures that could be targeted at the genuinely needy is limited thanks to the government's large fiscal deficit. The net result is that economic activity is bound to slow down. And though the precise extent of the slowdown is hard to predict, the fact that even the most conservative estimates do not place GDP growth at less than 6 per cent provides some solace.

REFERENCES

Henry, Peter Blair (2007), "Capital Account Liberalization: Theory, Evidence, and Speculation", *Journal of Economic Literature*, Vol. XLV, December.

IMF (2008b), "World Economic Outlook", October.

International Monetary Fund (2008a), *"Global Financial Stability Report"*, October.

Mohan, Rakesh (2006), "Coping With Liquidity Management in India: A Practitioner's View", *Reserve Bank of India Bulletin*, April.

Mohan, Rakesh (2007a), "Development of Financial Markets in India", Reserve Bank of India Bulletin, June.

Mohan, Rakesh (2007b), "India's Financial Sector Reforms: Fostering Growth While Containing Risk", *Reserve Bank of India Bulletin*, December.

Prasad, Eswar S., Raghuram G. Rajan and Arvind Subramanian (2007), "Foreign Capital and Economic Growth", *Brookings* Papers on *Economic Activity*, 1.

Reserve Bank of India (2008), *Annual Policy Statement for the Year 2008-09,* April, World Bank (2008), "Global Development Finance 2008", June.

CHAPTER

The Psychological Impact of Recession

Subhashree Panda

ABSTRACT

Recession has melted down economies, companies and now employee's health. According to a recent survey by ASSOCHAM, over half of the service sector people are suffering from diseases, caused due to stress and overwork. The full-blown recession has hit behavioral health hard. More people need help. Fewer can afford it. This is not the first time that the global economy is going through recession and this is also not the last time. There is a pattern involved in it. On an average it is happening after every 8-10 years. This article is an attempt to highlight the psychological effect of recession on employee health.

INTRODUCTION

Almost everybody today seems to be discussing about the U.S. recessionary trend and its impact on emerging countries, more particularly India. Economists, industrialists and the common man on the streets seem to have been horrified by the very thought of recession in India and that too due to U.S. Decreasing industrial production, inflation, decreasing job opportunities, cost cutting, reducing purchasing power parity, et al are the aspects discussed among them through every possible mode like articles, talks and walks and places like washrooms, canteens, etc.

It has become virtually impossible to ignore bad news about the economy. Every day, Americans are bombarded with reports of slumping stock markets, massive layoffs, and dismal business forecasts. Many are experiencing these phenomena first hand. And it's increasingly apparent that the constant onslaught of economic gloom and doom is not only impacting people's wallets - it's also affecting their psyches. Social workers and other professionals around the country report that the slowdown has put an enormous amount of pressure on their clients. For many clients, the stress is too much to handle. They are falling victim to anxiety and depression and trying to ease their fears with alcohol and other drugs. Such responses are not uncommon during times of economic turmoil, but the situation may be more dire this time around. There are signs that people are already cutting back or foregoing services in an attempt to save money or because they no longer have insurance coverage. Observers say they fear that if this skimping continues for an extended period, it will result in an eventual influx of people with major problems - an influx the system may not be able to handle. As time goes on, people's problems just fester. They get worse.

Dynamics Involved

In our life, there is a special place for money (be it in any currency). Most of the problems that we are facing in our life and day-to-day living are linked with it. Food, shelter, clothes, life-style, education, comforts and etc, each and everything involves money. Money should be revolving; it comes, it goes and it comes back again. It should always change hands or else it is useless. It is this nature of the money that drives the economy of a country, a company or our life. And when we are going through recession, it means no money is coming in. Money is not coming in but yet we need to live and hence there is a need for cost-cutting. But we never know how long the recession will continue and hence more cost cutting. People drive the economy and when there is recession then it is these very people who suffer and then you are laid off. Now what? What will you do? How will you survive? How will you take care of yourself and your family? Earlier there was less money coming in and now there is no money coming in, what will you do?

In such times of global recession when everyone is trying hard to survive and pass through one of the toughest phase of their life, no one thinks about making the profit out of adversity. Everyone is trying to survive and it will be survival of the fittest. Anyone who will be able to pass through this will come out as a stronger entity or person or country. Companies are no exception to this rule. They are also trying hard to survive. With them they are also trying to float and swim through as many people as possible but certainly not all. As a part of cost cutting, some of the employees need to be laid off, so that the company and others can survive. Similar things happens in a lift, when it is overloaded; ship, when it is sinking and even airplane, when it is overloaded and etc. Something or someone needs to go out for the rest of them to survive. But, what is the pattern? Who needs to be laid-off? When? How?

Survey on Impact of Recession on Employee Health and Integrity

- The most recent "American Workplace Insights" survey from Adecco Group North America gives great insight into the state of mind of America's workforce.
- The stresses and strains of the current economic situation have caused many Americans to consider unethical conduct on the job.
- In addition, a staggering number of Americans report that the recession has caused a negative impact on their mental health and develop unseen illnesses.
- a huge negative impact on morale and productivity at work.
- Coworkers' emotional suffering is "contagious."

- Employees working while mentally "absent" are often unproductive and may pose a safety threat.
- People often "self-medicate" in response to stress and depression, so increased drug and alcohol abuse among workforce is a significant possibility.
- Survey found that 28 per cent of people would do something dishonest to keep their jobs (examples included blaming co-workers for mistakes, blackmail, and flirting with a superior).
- Almost half of American workers (47%) expect their compensation to stay the same or decrease this year.
- Yet only 15 per cent said the current economic situation has impacted them personally by causing them to actively save for possible unemployment.
- Despite increasing lay-offs, a staggering 82 per cent say their employer is not paying more attention to their performance.

Struggling Financially, Struggling Mentally

Anecdotal evidence suggests that the recession is becoming a top reason why people are seeking mental health services. For example, several national insurance companies report that more people are using their employee assistance programs (EAPs). These programs offer employees a confidential way to access short-term counseling and connect with services such as child and elder care.

Philadelphia-based CIGNA Corporation has seen calls to its EAP climb 60% during the months following the financial collapse in the fall of 2008, says Doug Nemecek, MD, the insurer's national medical director. Representatives of Hartford, CT-based Aetna Inc. and Indianapolis-based WellPoint, Inc. say their companies also have seen increases. Not only is the number of calls to EAPs going up, the topics of conversation have shifted away from traditional issues such as marital stress and family discord to job troubles, struggles with mortgages, and financial stress. Clearly, there are people who have struggled with anxiety, depression, or substance abuse, and the economic crisis has made their problems worse.

Some people may find themselves being more irritable, anxious, lethargic or sad. Some may be unable to sleep, may eat too much or too little, or may experience physical symptoms of stress, like high blood pressure or headaches. Others may turn to behaviors like gambling, alcohol or drug use. Often, one symptom can lead to another - anxiety can lead to sleeplessness, which can cause greater stress and so on. There are a variety of suggested coping techniques and ways to get help, depending on the individual situation. In general, experts advise people to engage in activities that can release stress, such as exercise, hobbies or socializing with friends and family. Sharing worries with people experiencing similar stress can help.

More people also are reaching out to providers of community-based mental health services. Members of the New Jersey Association of Mental Health Agencies, Inc. have seen a roughly 20 per cent increase in demand for services since the late summer of 2008. Crisis calls are going up, and more people are reporting stress-related physical symptoms such as stomach ulcers and headaches. It's been busier for the staff of the Family Involvement Centre, a non-profit organisation in Arizona that helps families with children who have behavioral health needs. Many of the children the centre serves sense their caregivers' increased stress and are exhibiting more anxiety and frustration at home and in school, says Jane Kallal, the centre's executive director. At the same time, Boys and Girls Clubs of America and other nonprofits that traditionally provide recreational and educational outlets for youth have to cope with reduced donations, Kallal says. All of this compounds and does create more stress for the families," she says. It's a vicious cycle that we're in right now.

Changes have been felt in the world of substance abuse treatment as well. Until a few months ago, the majority of people seeking help at Townsend, a chain of outpatient facilities in the Southeast, had a primary diagnosis of prescription drug addiction. Now, the majority of new clients are addicted to alcohol. Alcohol is the current drug of choice because it's cheaper than other addictive substances, says Michael Handley, CEO of Destin, FL-based Townsend. Jodi Conway, LCADC, who runs a private practice in Dumont, NJ, says many of her clients are having trouble kicking their addictions or are relapsing because of financial stress. The effects aren't limited to patients with alcohol or drug addictions.

The downturn has renewed interest in research related to the psychological effects of financial stressors, particularly unemployment. Recent reports have linked job displacement and unemployment to lower rates of participation in social activities (Brand and Burgard, 2008), lower levels of mental health (Cassidy and Wright, 2008; Scutella and Wooden, 2008), and heavy drinking (Mossakowski, 2008). The psychological impact of unemployment can be deep and long lasting. Even though many people initially see unemployment as a chance for a new start, research done by Goldsmith (Goldsmith, Veum and Darity, 1997; Goldsmith, Veum and Darity, 1996) shows that optimism is often replaced by hopelessness, depression, anxiety, and low self-esteem as unemployment lingers. Employment is important to people psychologically because it gives us status, organizes our day, puts us in connection with other people, and gives us a purpose. When job has been taken away, it really jostles individual. One can really go into a deeper sense of psychological anguish.

Looking for New Ways to Cope

Many therapists encourage people to write down their worries and responsibilities before they go to bed, which can keep them from dwelling on them while they are trying to sleep. They also encourage people to try to take action or make decisions in areas where they have some control, like deciding whether it is affordable to send the children to camp this summer or deciding to cut back on dinners out or other expenses. And doing what one can to address financial problems or develop new job skills can make a person feel better able to handle economic uncertainty. Differentiate between real problems and making that problem worse by complicating it with other issues, such as a destructive relationship or using alcohol and drugs. That makes it worse. No situation so bad that one can't do something to make it worse.

Even though the need for mental health and substance abuse services has increased because of the recession, that doesn't mean all providers are seeing more patients. Financial difficulties are forcing many clients to choose cheaper, less-intensive forms of treatment. Mental health providers in Minnesota have seen more people asking about free medications and seek less-expensive alternatives, such as support groups, fitness classes, yoga, and meditation.

Some people are turning to the Internet for help. A few months ago, the Ruth Rales Jewish Family Service in Boca Raton, FL, launched several Web sites where people can go to receive counseling via e-mail. The organization decided to start the service to cater to the increasing number of people using the Internet to look for jobs and employment advice. The online counseling has attracted e-mails from people throughout the United States and Canada who are struggling with financial problems. His responses to these messages are designed to help people realize that they are not alone in their struggles and to remind them that they have strengths they can tap into to respond to crises. When one is counseling on the Internet, it brings more people to the process. That doesn't get someone a job, but it allows them to know that they are reacting in a very normal way to a very difficult situation.

As clients look for less-expensive services, social work practitioners who offer traditional in-person psychotherapy are trying to find ways to make their services more accessible to clients. Charles Rizzuto, a faculty member of the Smith College School for Social Work in Northampton, who also has a private practice, says he has had to become more flexible with how he charges and collects fees, even if that means he has less income. Similar trends are emerging in the substance abuse field. Conway says many of her patients are spacing out their appointments and relying more on 12-step programs. Wiedemann-West says her organization's outpatient business has picked up in recent months while demand for its residential services has declined. Insurers are more likely to pay for outpatient treatment, and people are increasingly averse to leaving their workplaces for inpatient treatment, she says. People are afraid to leave their jobs for an extended period of time and don't want their employers to consider them 'out of sight, out of mind.

Concern for the Future

A prolonged economic slowdown could have disastrous consequences for people struggling with mental health problems and addictions. Many people who cannot afford to access the services their need will eventually enter the system when they are much sicker or even suicidal. And it's unlikely that states—many of which are facing multibillion-dollar deficits—will be able or willing to provide more funding for services. Some observers are hoping that President Obama's administration may kick-start the economy and provide the impetus for fundamental reform that will make mental health and substance abuse services more affordable and accessible. Yet, it is unlikely that any changes will happen soon. No matter what happens, the downturn has at least raised the public's awareness of the importance of social workers' role in helping people struggling with mental illness and addiction.

Conclusion

We cannot control the economy. We cannot control the pressures placed on world markets by the exploding middle classes of India and China. We are, without doubt, at the sufferance of a juggernaut that we ourselves have created. We can choose to manage ourselves in the face of what amounts to a global crisis. We can choose to recognize that all things occur in cycles and that, while our current situation may be deeply distressing, it will change. It may not change in exactly the way we expect or would like, but it will change. And change always provides us with an opportunity - it is not an obstacle. We can also choose not to live in fear and not to let the momentary influences that surround us change who we are and how we behave. Pain - whether emotional or physical—has the effect of causing us to act out of character. This gauntlet that we are all facing is a time for increasing our self-awareness, attending to the things that feed us rather than bleed us, for taking stock and taking responsibility for our own personal universe.

Take a lesson—take care of yourself and take care those around you.

REFERENCES

Brand, J. E., and Burgard, S. A. (2008). Job displacement and social participation over the lifecourse: Findings for a cohort of joiners. *Social Forces*, 87(1), pp. 211-242.

Cassidy, T., and Wright, L. (2008). Graduate employment status and health: A longitudinal analysis of the transition from student. *Social Psychology of Education*, 11(2), pp.181-191.

Goldsmith, A. H., Veum, J. R., and Darity, W. (1996). The psychological impact of unemployment and joblessness. *Journal of Socio-Economics*, 25(3), pp. 333-358.

Goldsmith, A. H., Veum, J. R., and Darity, W. (1997). Unemployment, joblessness, psychological well-being and self-esteem: Theory and evidence. *Journal of Socio-Economics*, 26(2), pp. 133-158.

Mossakowski, K. N. (2008). Is the duration of poverty and unemployment a risk factor for heavy drinking? *Social Science & Medicine*, 67(6),pp. 947-955.

Scutella, R., and Wooden, M. (2008). The effects of household joblessness on mental health. *Social Science & Medicine*, 67(1), pp. 88-100.

Index

D

E

F

G

❑❑❑